Toasts and Tributes

TITLE PAGE BY W. C. BAMBURGH

DECORATIONS BY J. SINRAMM

Toasts and Tributes

A Happy Book of Good Cheer Good Health Good Speed Devoted to the Blessings and Comforts of Life South of the Stars

Edited by Arthur Gray

New York
Rohde and Haskins
MCMIV

Republished by Omnigraphics • 615 Griswold Street • Detroit • 2000

THE WINTHROP PRESS
NEW YORK

COPYRIGHT
1904
ROHDE & HASKINS

Library of Congress Cataloging-in-Publication Data

Toasts and tributes : a happy book of good cheer, good health, good speed, devoted to the blessings and comforts of life south of the stars / edited by Arthur Gray.
    p.   cm.
Originally published : New York : Rhode and Haskins, 1904.
Includes index.
ISBN 0-7808-0305-1 (alk. paper)
1. Toasts. I. Gray, Arthur.
PN6341.T62   1999
808.5'1—dc21   99-15291
                                  CIP

Printed in the United States of America

To the enthusiasts of good living this book is devoted in the hope that they may find enough in these pages to make them feel at home.

As for Toasts and Sentiments,
they are to be looked upon, we
suppose as a necessity — a con-
cession to human weakness.
                    —the Nation.

Foreword

THERE is a reason for this little book, and
the reason is that every man and woman has
a leaning towards material blessings. Everybody
has an interest in the works of human nature
and the good things of earth.

For all such enthusiasts of life this book is
intended, in the hope that they may find much of
the best that is worth toasting presented in these
pages. To those who have missed in this work a
toast or a tribute to those attributes of our spiritual
and mental existence, namely, Love, Truth, Character, Courage, Sympathy and their kindred, it may
be said that these qualities are embodied to a greater
or less degree in the other subjects named. These
features of the mind and soul are inherited and
developed by our fathers, mothers, sweethearts
and wives. Poetry, Music and Art possess divine
elements. A soothing and comforting smoke is
worthy of a song. Does not good Gambrinus move
in the best circles? Yes, indeed, my masters!

The three great mysteries, Life, Sleep and Death,
have also been omitted. That which has been

done so wisely by writers whose works are known and accessible to us all must give us pause.

For the above reason no toast or tribute to the scheme of creation and its ruling forces—Sun, Moon, Stars—has been entered in this volume.

In brief, this book is intended to deal with the social and domestic relations of life. It is designed to be earthy; not of the grovelling earth, but of the earth which gives us its blessings; blessings which richly deserve these toasts and tributes.

Contents

Contents

Subject and Title Index

A

C

Subject and Title Index

E

[17]

G

Subject and Title Index

I

M

Subject and Title Index

P

R

S

[28]

T

The Origin of Toasts

AS the creation of any custom having a social or sentimental significance has been rarely traced to its author, it is not strange that we cannot locate the original "toaster."

The history of manners and customs shows that the Romans were among the early nations to use a piece of toasted bread in wine when they drank to each other's "healths," and as "toast" is of Latin derivation,—from Tostus, bread dried or scorched before the fire—there can be little doubt that the Romans first applied the *word* in the above sense.

Any custom, unless it is recognized at once as vital to the health and prosperity of a people, is not copied slavishly by one nation from another. It is not singular, therefore, that while the Romans adhered to their sentiments and Cæsar may have carried their fashion of "drinking healths" into Great Britain, the British—never influenced by the ways of other nations—did not adopt this custom according to the Roman book.

In spite of the ancient Roman connection with the word "toasts" and its application to their festivities, the following is to be found in an old English publication: "While it must be admitted that the origin of the word toast is very doubtful indeed, the ladies—it may not be out of place to remark—have, in drinking healths, a modern way of excusing themselves, thus felicitously described by Goldsmith in his delightful poem, 'The Deserted Village':

'Nor the coy maid, half willing to be prest,
Shall kiss the cup to pass it to the rest.' "

As sentiment has existed, however, since the beginning of time—long before there were any "great men" or "mutual admiration societies," to whom tributes could be paid—who could or would wish to deny that the original toast was the ardent impulse of a loin-girded youth who seeing for the first time the reflection of a maiden in a crystal stream, sought to drown himself in the illusion, but, failing, drank to her health in passionate tributes from his horn cup; for it was a woman, surely, who inspired the first toast.

[34]

Perhaps it was the radiant, stately and com-
pelling Aspasia who, at her first banquet, moved
the guests of Pericles to deep and long libations in
praise of her beauty and power.

Perhaps it was some Olympic god who raised
his golden goblet to Aphrodite, or some Greek lover
to Sappho.

Perhaps—but we can weave our own fancies for
legendary, mythological and historical heroines.

No legend in song or story, revealing the source
of this charming custom, has come down to us
through the ages; no lyric in impassioned metre
to vaunt the brimming cup.

The custom of drinking toasts dates back to a
period previous to the mediæval times, when the
loving-cup was still regarded as an indispensable
feature of every banquet. The ceremony attend-
ing this sentiment was as follows:

The cup would be filled to the brim with wine or
mead, in the center of which would be placed a
piece of toasted bread. The host, after putting
his lips to the cup, would pass it to the guest of
honor, seated on his right hand; the latter would in
turn pass it to his right hand neighbor, until
finally the cup would come back to the host, who
would drain what remained and swallow the piece
of toast in honor of all the friends assembled at

the table. History teaches that the ancient Greeks and Romans, the Assyrians and the Egyptians were in the habit of drinking one another's health at dinner. Indeed, at Athens, the etiquette concerning what may be described as the liquid courtesies of this kind was very strict and elaborate, being known by the name of "Philothesis." The participants of the repast were in the habit of drinking to one another until they could carry no more, and then they would pour the remainder of the wine on the altar of any pagan deity that happened to be handy. At Rome the same custom prevailed. Post-prandial oratory was severely condemned as out of place; and while the Greeks contented themselves with exclaiming as they put the wine to their lips, "I salute you, be happy," the Romans restricted themselves to the exclamation, "Propino," which is the Latin for "I drink your health."

When England began to emerge from her semi-barbaric state and took upon herself a social system, "healths in honor of mortals" was one of her importations. Many fine stories and happy incidents grew out of the use and abuse of the custom. One of the prettiest stories in this connection is told of Rowena, daughter of Hengist, the Saxon ally of the British king Vortigern.

Vortigern was being entertained by Hengist for the purpose of making him his son-in law, and then destroying him. After dinner the ladies were admitted and Rowena was at the head of them. She carried aloft a capacious goblet of wine, and approaching the dazzled and delighted Vortigern, said with reverence: "Lord King, I drink to your health." This was said in Saxon, and Vortigern shook his head to show that he had not been taught that language and was very sorry for it.

He looked inquiringly at his interpreter, and although that official translated the lady's words, their meaning was lost on Vortigern.

As Rowena stood silently gazing at him, cup in hand, he found himself in a condition that required a master of ceremonies. "What ought I to do?" he asked of his interpreter. The latter replied: "As the lady has offered to drink your health, saying 'Wacht Heil,' you should bid her quaff the wine, saying, 'Drinck Heil.'" Vortigern shaped his British mouth to the utterance of the foreign idiom, and Rowena smiled so exquisitely at his uncouth accent, before she kissed the brim of the cup, that the king lost his head and heart and speedily became doubly drunk with love and wine.

Thus drinking of healths was brought into Britain, and under such distinguished patronage that it became a universal fashion, and it had a pretty conclusion attached to it, which in later degenerate days went out with the fashion itself. The gallant Vortigern, when he returned the Saxon lady's compliment, and took the cup to drink, not only quaffed it to her health, but before he did so kissed her rose-tinted lips with such fervor that the custom of giving healths was at once firmly established, and when a lady drank to a gentleman, the latter not only pledged her the formulary of "Drinck Heil" but saluted her lips.

Another interesting story, bearing on the subject, tells of a beautiful Bath, England, maiden who, some time in the seventeenth century, when, according to the fashion of the times, it was customary to bathe publicly in rich dresses designed for the purpose, received a liquid ovation while she was displaying her grace of figure and charm of costume. One admirer took a goblet of the water in which she stood and drank to her health. Another enthusiast, stimulated by less innocuous libations, expressed his desire to possess the subject of the toast, and swore that, while he cared not for the liquor, he would have the toast—meaning the lady herself. He was restrained from his caprice, but the custom of drinking to the health of woman found permanent favor after that incident.

Long before this period, in fact, as early as the middle of the sixteenth century, sack and punch were drunk with toasted bread. Between leisurely bites and sips, many verbal bouquets were thrown to hosts and hostesses under the influence of friendly cups.

The almost universal prevalence of conviviality in the seventeenth century naturally spread the custom. Drinking healths became not merely a fashion, but a habit. On those occasions the unmarried woman of beauty and talent was especially favored. It also became the custom to designate as a "toast" the woman whose health was so drunk. The incident of the Lady of the Bath was originally applied in this sense.

First to beauty and her train, therefore, were the cups lifted highest; beauty, then valor, then a toast on any occasion when the wine of enthusiasm and gratitude flowed.

Out of this custom grew those silent tributes when nothing but the divine voice of the poet could interpret the highest human impulses.

Toasts and tributes:—Toasts within the walls of fine fellowships; tributes, ringing, graceful and sincere, from the pens of grateful writers; the easy chair, the fireside, the open window, the glories of nature, the playthings of childhood, the diversions of youth, the absorptions of maturity and the reflections of old age; the creature comforts that divert and uplift; that restrain the mind from brooding; in short, the promoters of content that soothe us physically, strengthen us mentally, and better us spiritually; to everything animate and inanimate which has contributed to our well-being; the Book of Life, teeming with recollections, reflections and memories; to these, and all other environing blessings of life, we yield affectionate homage. ARTHUR GRAY.

The Toast-Master

A BRIGHT diner-out once said that the duty of the toast-master is to "keep sober and offend nobody." While this may be a broad definition of his responsibilities, it by no means covers the ground. The first requisite for a successful toast-master is TACT. He must know, intuitively, when to call upon the heavy-weight orator who will serve his information in solid slices, when to introduce the dainty wit who adds spice to the "feast of reason" and when to bring on the buffoon who furnishes the guffaws which aid digestion. The toast-master, like the poet, must "be born"; he can't be made. No amount of suggestion, no set rules can make a good toast-master; he need not be an eloquent speaker, he need not be a brilliant wit—in fact, it is better that he should be neither —but he must be a man thoroughly sure of himself, quick-witted enough to formulate his ideas on his feet, with sufficient self-confidence to express them gracefully, and with enough saving good sense to be willing to efface himself.

The toast-master is like the flour in a plum-pudding—he is necessary to hold all the other good things together, but the moment he predominates and thrusts himself forward at the expense of the plums, the citron and the spices, he becomes a nuisance—and he spoils the pudding.

It has become a fashion, in these latter years, for the toast-master to introduce speakers with some flippant remarks or, popularly expressed, "roasts"; this method is safe in the hands of an artist—or a born toast-master—but it is fatal when attempted by the average man. The late Moses P. Handy, founder and for many years president of the famous Clover Club, at whose dinners more distinguished men have spoken than at any other organization in the country, was an expert in this line. I remember, when, one night, as we finished our coffee, he arose and remarked: "There are certain rules prescribed by etiquette which even the Clover Club cannot ignore. We have, with us this evening, several distinguished visitors to whom we must listen before the enjoyment of the evening begins. Chief Justice ——— of the Supreme Court will now say a few words." It is but fair to say for Chief Justice ———

that he "made good" in a rattling speech which cap- tured even the jaded epicures of the Clover Club. Joe Howard, for several years President of the New York Press Club and its most successful toast-master, is another who uses impudence, insolence, almost insult, so deftly that, coming from his lips, the most outre expressions sound like compliments. But geniuses like these are unsafe examples for the average man to follow.

The unaccustomed toast-master should remember that it is the other fellow's wit and wisdom, not his, that the guests come to hear.

He is, to an extent, in the position of host of the intellectual banquet, and while it is permissible for him to extol some of the more notable mental viands he offers, it is in distinctly bad taste for him to decry their quality. Your toast-master should no more criticise the ability of his speakers than your host should abuse the flavor of his soup. If he knew them to be bad, he is insulting you by placing them before you. "Roasts" of a speaker is a cheap way of gaining a laugh, at best, and, if the speaker is clever, it may be a boomerang which returns by getting the laugh on the toast-master.

While, at most dinners, the programme is laid out beforehand, the toast-master has a certain latitude, and he should try "to take off the cruelty," as the

Irish say, of a serious speech, by calling upon some-one who will talk in a lighter vein. Two instructive addresses in succession at a dinner are in as bad taste as two heavy roasts on the menu; no good maître d'hôtel or toast-master will permit either.

While it requires infinite tact, quick wit and peculiar adaptability to make an ideal toast-master, almost any man with good sense, fair speaking ability and a sense of what is fitting from him to his guests, as the host of the intellectual banquet, can conduct a dinner with dignity and decorum. One rule might be laid down as an axiom: The less the toast-master obtrudes his own personality the more suc-cessful he will be as toast-master.

ALLAN FORMAN.

The After-Dinner Mastodon

Post-prandial Philosophy by the Editor of
"The Schoolmaster"

AFTER-DINNER speaking is the art of saying nothing briefly.

To realize the passage of time—that is the very summit and exaltation of after-dinner genius, rarely reached—it seems—even by those many gentlemen who are presumed to be great. How seldom a dinner runs smoothly! Whose fault is it?

The toast-master should be an autocrat—a very czar in his high seat—but he should not attempt to exercise his authority, as odd numbers of toast-masters do, in monopolizing time.

To be a toast-master in these days is a task that many men undertake with daring and few accomplish with satisfaction. The desire to talk on the

[45]

part of the toast-master is frequently far more intense than the craving of some of the after-dinner hypnotists themselves.

Your toast-master should be an artist; in introducing the speaker he should make a rough, true sketch of the victim and present him quickly to the crowd.

In fact, my friend, be a Master of the toasts and not a biographer; be the soul of the feast and inspire the audience at once with the fact that you know how to handle those who have been invited—or hired—to speak.

Don't weary the audience and don't permit any one else to weary it. Prolonging the programme until everybody is tired out kills the very best dinner that the cook can serve. Begin it and end it with a snap. Let the company break up reluctantly, clamoring for more.

The dinner table is no place for the delivery of long public lectures. It is the place where men meet for pleasure; what they want is relaxation; entertainment, not torture.

Those who do not recognize this should not be recognized. At a Lincoln dinner, several years ago, a distinguished lawyer and orator from the West, delivered a magnificent after-dinner lecture—one hour and a half long—on the life of Lincoln. Six hundred gentlemen at the tables became nervous wrecks, and the ladies, in the galleries, looked down upon the great test of endurance in horror and amazement.

Finally the orator stopped and the exhausted audience wondered what other punishment would follow when the next speaker came upon the stage; but the first sentence he uttered gave the crowd the relief it craved. He said: "Ladies and gentlemen, the orator who preceded me would have been famous had he died in the middle of his speech."

The speeches should be as dainty as the dishes.

Serve them quickly, remove them rapidly.

The after-dinner mastodon should be suppressed.

You have no right to confine a crowd of people in a room where they are chained by courtesy and custom and hold them at the mercy of speakers who are like human phonographs charged with Edison records or like ventriloquized mummies, dead but not buried. If you cannot be brilliant be brief.

Win, sirs, a reputation at least for being kind. Gods! but it is a sign of stupidity or Olympian vanity that a man shall talk when no one wants to hear him. Toast-master, do your duty. Try to avoid this sorrow at the start, but if it comes, let one perish that many may survive.

CRESWELL MACLAUGHLIN.

Toasts and Tributes

By WALLACE IRWIN

*Author of "Love Sonnets of a Hoodlum," "Rubaiyat
of Omar Khayyam, Jr.," etc.*

TO THE AFTER-DINNER SPEECH

Come, touch your glasses overhead
To what we love, to what we dread;
    The after-dinner speech.
Oh, may it come when we are strong,
Its length be short, its laughs be long,
    Its flights within our reach.

Oh, may the speaker's stories smack
Of something more than almanack
    And less than vaudeville;
And may the wight who comes this way
With nothing—or too much—to say,
    In heaven's name, keep still!

A TOAST BY PROXY

I used to know a clever toast,
    But pshaw! I cannot think it—
So fill your glass to Anything
    And, bless your souls, I'll drink it.

A NAVAL TOAST

If a hostile foreign rag
Floats above our nation's flag,
    Pull it down!
But if foreign gentlemen
Join our friendly tipple, then
    Drink it down!

If a warlike foreign fleet
Comes our battleships to meet,
    Fill the cup!
And we'll gladly drink their navy
To the watery depths o' Davy—
    Bottoms up!

TO KISSES

I pledge the kiss
Whose poignant bliss
Comes from a microbe, so they say.
    A microbe?—ho!
    If that is so
He tickles in a pleasant way.

"And faith," say I,
"If man must die
Of microbe that and microbe this,
    I'll gladly sip
    The fatal lip,
And take my microbe in a kiss."

A FAT MAN'S TOAST

A toast to us, my good round friends,
　　To bless the things we eat;
For it has been full many a year
　　Since we have seen our feet.
Yet who would lose a precious pound
　　By trading sweets for sours?
It takes a mighty girth indeed
　　To hold such hearts as ours!

A TOAST FROM GERMANY

To vomankind I raise mein stein
　　Und trink avay der pubbles.
She is der cause of care und shtrife,
Der greatest foolishness in life,
　　Und himmel! such a troubles!

She chabs you mit an angry vord
　　Ven you are talking friend-wise,
Und ven she gits ein spieling fit
So kvick she speag your chance is nit
　　To git ein vord in end-wise.

If vimmen vere not lifing here,
　　Choost men residing only,
Ve all vould feel a great release,
Mit guietness, und rest, und peace—
　　Ach gott! it vould be lonely!

[51]

TO ADAM AND EVE

Here's to the Garden of Eden
Which Adam was always a-weedin'
    Till Eve by mistake
    Got bit up by a snake
Who on the ripe pippins was feedin'.

Then a longing it seemed to possess her
For clothing sufficient to dress her;
    And ever since then
    It's been up to us men
To pay for her dresses—God bless her!

TO THE SUMMER GIRL

Summer girl, with cheeks of tan,
Blessings on thee, little man!

With your merry, whistled lore
And your turned up—pompadour.

May some seaside lover true
Soon turn up and marry you!

He is welcome, if he can—
Blessings on him, little man!

A ST. PATRICK'S DAY TOAST

Sure, here's a long dhrink to St. Pathrick,
    An' wan to Jarge Washington, too,
For Jarge war the b'y who could not tell a lie—
    And Pathrick told only a few.

For Jarge war as thruthful as daylight
    An' hatin' all liars an' fakes,
An' Pat shpoke as thrue as Jarge Wash'nton, too—
    Till he started to talk about shnakes!

TO A "PLUNGER"

May you make the largest fortune,
    May you own the finest yacht,
May you rear the highest building
    On the finest building lot;
May you run the swiftest auto,
    Which you manage with such skill
That the roads are fairly scattered
    With the victims that you kill.

TO THE SIMPLE LIFE

Here's to the native of Pungaloo
    Who rests all day from labor,
Who, when he's hungry for a stew,
    Goes out and kills a neighbor.
He worries not about the style
    That gentlefolk should foller:
He merely wears a happy smile,
    A sunburn and a collar.

[53]

TO EVERYBODY

Here's good luck to everyone, black, white or yellow,
Hard hearted villain or jolly good fellow,
Drunken or sober, or foolish or wise,
Angel incog. or knave in disguise,
Priest who for lonesome celibacy strives,
Holy old Mormon with forty-nine wives,
Sleepy old fogy or hustle-or-bust,
Magnate or delegate, union or trust,
Good, bad, indifferent, shady or light,
Fill up your glasses and send 'em off right.

TO THE TRUSTS

Here's to the Trusts which are not dead as yet,
For the longer you curse 'em the stronger they get.

So if we would strangle their dragon-like breath
Let's try a new method and bless 'em to death.

TO THE POETS

Then a health to the Poets I'll toss,
    To Byron and Shelley and Keats,
To Dobson the blithe and Swinburne the lithe
    And the Irish phenomenon, Yeats;
Then pausing a moment on earth,
    I'll fill up my glass to the brim
To the metrical flow of Miss Phœbe Snow
    And that breakfast food bard, Sunny Jim.

Toasts and Tributes

By JOHN ERNEST McCANN

LIFE

Here's to Life: entered with a protest—endured on compulsion—and left with a sigh.

DAME AND MISS FORTUNE

Here's to Miss Fortune—may we always Miss her.
Here's to Dame Fortune—may we meet and kiss her.

SWEETHEARTS

Here's to Sweethearts: the morning-glories of life, the first real flowers that we gather in the garden of existence.

THE OLD MAID

Here's to the poor old Maid:
    May she know in heaven the bliss
She missed here, because afraid
    To be awakened with a kiss.

LOVE

" 'Tis better to have loved and lost,"
Than to marry and be bossed.

WIVES

Here's to Wives: the apples of the soul, and may you never throw away the cores.

THE WOMAN

Here's to the woman of thirty-and-five:
She's as sweet as the Queen Bee throned in her hive.
She's worth all the maidens of "bashful fifteen"
That ever were thought of, heard of, or seen!

BABIES

Here's to Babies: the buds of humanity; the rulers of mothers; the employers of fathers; the despots of households; the criers in the night; the blessings of the day; but for whom the sun would shine, the stars gleam, the winds whisper, the waters flow, upon, to, and through a deserted world.

WOMAN AND BABY

Here's to Woman, the pilot, and Baby, the compass, of your barque:
They will steer you into morning, through the fog, the storm and dark.

THE BIBLE

Here's to the Bible: the most magnificent series of comedies and tragedies known to man.

BOYS

Here's to Boys: the destroyers of dignity; the demolishers of conceit; the annihilators of self-esteem; the detectors of sham; the champions of merit; the scoffers of the false; the boomers of the true; the bête-noirs of policemen; the protectors of sisters; the sweethearts of mothers; the champions and chums of good fathers; the Apaches of the streets; the law-breakers of to-day; the law-makers of to-morrow; the builders of cities; the constructors of nations.

LIES

Here's to Lies—when they protect the defenseless, the weak and the good from misery, death and the wicked.

TRUTH

Here's that it may never be told—except in a good cause.

GIRLS

Here's to Girls: the Easter Lilies of the world, whose fragrance alone would make "life worth living" in Siberia.

MOTHERS

Here's to Mothers: and in heaven may their children always be babies.

THE ACTOR

Here's to the Actor: who, no matter what character he plays, can never hide his own.

THE DRAMA

Here's to the Drama: the greatest force for good since the Bible.

THE CRITIC

Here's to the Critic: who is blind to only his own shortcomings.

THE EDITOR

Here's to the Editor: May he live long on expectations and short on copy; may he never find pen or blue pencil when eager to cut a good manuscript while the presses wait; may he never read good copy when half full of Rhinewine, and may Saint Peter be off on a long vacation when he arrives at The Gate.

POETS

Here's to Poets: the stars of a nation's flag and character, without whom, no matter how rich, nations are poor.

LANDLADIES

Here's to Landladies: and may they all have hall-rooms in—heaven.

THE MILLIONAIRE

Here's to the Millionaire—the noblest work of— the Trusts.

EVERY MAN

Here's to every man who is an I. O. U. to his country.

AMERICA

Here's to America, from the Arctic Circle to Cape Horn.

TROUBLE

Here's trouble to those who look across the Atlantic from foreign shores for it.

PROSPERITY

Here's to Prosperity, and may it be given the freedom of every town on our continent.

OUR CHINESE WALL

Here's to our Chinese Wall, and forever may it stand, a terror to the pirates and bandits of Europe —the Monroe Doctrine.

[59]

BASEBALL

Here's to our National Game, Baseball, the best tonic sent by the Lord in forty years to brace and support a nation.

POLICEMEN

Here's to Policemen: the foreign rulers of the American citizen.

THE EAGLE

Here's to the Irish-Jewish-German-American Eagle—as the old original seems to be dead.

OUR RULERS

God bless the President, Governor and Mayor— if they are worth blessing.

PARIS

Here's to Paris: the City of Grisettes, and the Grisette of Cities.

THE WORLD

Here's to the World: and may an Edison some day find out what in the World it was made for.

ROAST BEEF

Roast Beef! to thee I sing,
  Thou royal health-defender!
Thou rich and juicy thing,
  So warm, and sweet, and tender!
Thou bulwark of the heart,
  And of the soul the captor,
Whene'er—where'er—thou art,
  Of life thou art a factor!

Roast Beef! thy juices flow
  Around the stomach's portals.
They've raised men lying low
  To soar with the immortals!
Roast Beef! this song I sing
  To honor and to greet thee:
Thou democratic thing,
  King and peasant eat thee!

Toasts and Tributes

By CRESWELL MACLAUGHLIN

REAL GREATNESS

Engrave this sentiment on your soul—that unselfish love for mankind has been the inspiration of all great statesmen.

THE PAYROLL

The payroll is the bottom of business, and when that stops the bottom drops out.

MONEY

Here's to Money: it gives manners even to pirates.

ENEMIES

Here's to our enemies, most of whom are in our head.

COURTESY

Here's to Courtesy. It is the oil of controversy. It keeps gentlemen who disagree from punching each other.

THE UNKNOWN QUANTITY

Here's to your man that says nothing—he is an unknown quantity. But your man that says too much is a quantity not worth knowing.

THE UNITED STATES

Our Southern lass has kissed her Northern lover
and the honeymoon is at hand. Prosperity smiles
upon the union. Husbandmen of peace have long
been at work.

TO THE PEDAGOGUE

You may couple the brains of Bacon
  With the enterprise of a bee,
But you'll lose your job in the public school
  If your trousers bag at the knee.

POLITICS

One hot bottle at his feet,
  One cold bottle at his head—
Such is the strenuous way
  Great statesmen go to bed.

OUR BEST PARTNERS

To the good wife who is a good doctor, a good
banker, and a good lawyer, to the man she loves,
and to the home which she alone makes beautiful.

WRITER'S CRAMP

A toast to the writer's cramp, from which few
brilliant writers suffer.

TO THE TAILOR

Here's to the tailor who builds our clothes, for he
knows, as well as we, that there is much in the design
of a man, not only in his shape, but in his intention.

[63]

TO OUR ENEMIES

The man who is not brave enough to make an enemy will not be brave enough to make a friend— and is poor stuff anyway.

TO THE YOUNGSTERS

Let us salute the children and remember that we were a child once, and some of us are perhaps one now.

THE ARMY OF CHILDHOOD

Armed with histories, their banners emblazoned with hope, advancing like a splendid army, the children of the public school march at the head of the human race, leading mankind forward to universal brotherhood. The conquest of the world is at hand and the battlefield is the mind of a child.

EDUCATION

Here's to Education. You can lead a man to college, but you cannot make him think.

TO YOUR MR. MICAWBERS

The man who waits for things to turn up has his eyes fixed on his toes.

OUR LITTLE WORLD

Here's to this little world of ours, which is not growing worse to the men and women who are doing their best to make it better.

[64]

TO A SWEETHEART

Sing me a song of love, my lass,
   And fill my heart, like a bowl,
With the wine that leaps to thy golden lips
   From the fountain of thy soul—
For never a bird in the life of spring
   Had ever a mate like mine,
And never a lass in the age of Love
   Had a braver heart than thine.

TO THE EARLY BIRD

'Tis an adage as ancient as Adam—
But not as old as the sun—
   That the earliest birds
   Don't gather in herds,
They get there one by one.
Now the motive of that is certain
   And the moral of this is true—
If you want to succeed
You must take the lead,
   And the crowd will follow you.

THE RIGHT SORT OF A FELLOW

You may know the fellow
   Who thinks he thinks,
Or the fellow who thinks he knows;
But find the fellow
   Who knows he thinks—
And you know the fellow who knows.

[65]

BRACE UP

Brace up, old man, never despair;
　　Life has some joys in it yet—
You may never be rich, you may never be great,
But carry your head like a ruler of state—
　　Don't sorrow, don't grumble, don't fret.

WILD-FLOWER

I wooed a wild-flower
　　On a day,
Along the roadway of my life;
　　I caught it ere it blew away
And kept it for a wife;
None ever caught a fairer flower,
　　None ever kissed a sweeter wife;
Than that within my pretty bower,
　　Than thou, my wild-flower wife.

TO THE LOVE-SPRING

Drink long and deep, dear mortal,
　　Of that sweet fount which flows
'Twixt earth and heaven's portal—
　　Oh! drink—while the love-spring flows.

PHILADELPHIA

All hail the tranquil village!
　　May nothing jar its ease,
Where spiders build their bridges
　　From the trolleys to the trees.

WALL STREET

The Bull and the Bear get mad in the ring
  And bellow and toss and tear,
The stocks go up when the Bull's on top
  And down they go with the Bear.
So what's the use of going to school
  And crowding the brain with cares,
When life is all scramble and glutton and gamble
  When men are all Bulls and Bears.

LINES TO AN ORATORICAL CHEST

Colonel Chest is a man we all admire,
  For his infinite wonderful wit;
He can talk ten hours in a gale of wind,
  And it never tires him a bit.

[67]

Toasts and Tributes

By HENRY STANLEY HASKINS

THE POSTMAN

Here's to the Postman; beautiful are his feet when he brings glad tidings.

BUTCHER BOY

Here's to the Butcher Boy; who carries a nation's strength on his arm.

BOOTBLACKS

Here's to Bootblacks; may they always take a shine to us.

TAILORS

Here's to Tailors; may they be needleless in Heaven.

UNDERTAKERS

Here's to Undertakers; may they never overtake us.

THE SUMMER GIRL

Here's to the Summer Girl; may she hibernate in Winter.

[68]

MONEY

Here's to Money; for spreading content through what it can't buy.

CARFARE

Here's to the humble "nickel," the foe of shoemakers.

POLITICS

Here's to Politics; the stimulus of Patriotism.

STARS AND STRIPES

Here's to our flag; which never sees a sunset.

MAN

Here's to Man; when he is one.

WOMAN

Here's to Woman; the salt of the earth since Lot's time.

BOYS

Here's to Boys; may they live to look back on themselves with envy.

GIRLS

Here's to Girls; wise and otherwise.

SWEETHEARTS

Here's to Sweethearts; be they Mothers, Sisters, or Wives.

[69]

MIRRORS

Here's to Mirrors; may we never avoid them.

HOBBIES

Here's to Hobbies; may they never need a veterinary.

HATS

Here's to Hats; the hotbeds of sedition and conspiracy and the sanctuaries of noble thoughts.

SHOES

Here's to Shoes; may more be worn out on the top rungs of the ladder.

WINTER

Here's to Winter; may we always be coaled.

A TRIBUTE TO GOLFERS

There was a man in our town,
  And he was wondrous wise.
He jumped into a tournament
  And came out with a prize.
And when he saw the cup he'd won,
  With all his might and main,
He jumped into ten entry lists
  But never won again.

THE KISS THAT BURNS

Oh! the kiss that burns,
And the bliss that yearns,
  'Neath the glowing evening star;
And the vows of love,
Touched by boughs above,
  Where the dreaming birdlets are.

Oh! the vagrant hour
In the fragrant bower
  (How I love you, my sweet coquette!)
Oh! the kiss that burns,
And the bliss that yearns,
  When I puff you—my cigarette.

THE TRAMP'S TOAST

Some toast the home and friendship's bond.
And some of family trees are fond.
They're not for me—my way I beat,
And trample *ties* beneath my feet.

BOYHOOD

The poets may sing of tobacco;
  Of "long-cut," "perique" and their ilk.
But give me the pleasure, forbidden,
  The first boyish whiff of corn-silk.

[71]

TENNIS

Here's to the service that twists like a snake;
  The volleying stroke in its might;
The cross-court return and the back-handed drive;
  The lob with its meteor flight.
And here's to the swish of the wind through the
    strings;
  The balls as they hurdle the net;
And here's to the spring of the turf 'neath the feet;
  In the strife of the deuce-vantage set.

The Human Family

Arms and the man I sing
>—*Virgil*

MAN

Men are rare.
>—*Florian*

Men are but great children.
>—*Napoleon*

Men are not to be measured by inches.
>—*Taunton*

Man is the circled oak; woman the ivy.
>—*Aaron Hill*

What a piece of work is a Man! how noble in reason! how infinite in faculty! in form and moving how express and admirable! in action how like an angel! in apprehension how like a god!
>—*Shakespeare*

Man is the merriest species of the creatures; all above and below are serious.
>—*Addison*

Man is a jewel of God, who has created the material world to keep his treasures in.

—*Theodore Parker*

Man is a plant, not fixed in the earth, not immovable, but heavenly; whose head, rising as it were from a root upwards, is turned towards heaven.

—*Plutarch*

Here's to Man from morning till night,
Here's to the Man with courage to fight,
The courage to fight and the courage to live—
The courage to learn, and to love and forgive.

—*Pseud.*

Fond man! the vision of a moment made!
Dream of a dream! and shadow of a shade!

—*Young*

Every man is valued in this world as he shows by his conduct that he wishes to be valued.

—*La Bruyère*

Here's to man's collars and cuffs and stiff shirt fronts; to his raiment generally; to his hat, whether felt or silk, wide brimmed or narrow; to his shoes—may they always guide his feet aright! Lastly, but not less chiefly, here's to man himself, any old thing in dress and body, but of necessity tall and broad shouldered and well groomed, mentally, and morally, and spiritually.

—*Henry Stanley Haskins*

Man is a noble animal, splendid in ashes and pompous in the grave.

—*Thomas Browne*

[74]

But we are all men,
In our own natures frail; and capable
Of our flesh; few are angels.
—*Shakespeare*

Man hath his daily work of body or mind
Appointed, when declares his dignity,
And the regard of heav'n on all his wings;
While other animals unactive range
And of their doing God takes no account.
—*Milton*

A man of knowledge increaseth strength.
—*Old Testament*

HONEST FRIEND

Here's a bottle and an honest friend!
  What wad you wish for mare, man?
Wha kens before his life may end
  What his share may be o' care, man?
—*Robert Burns*

Thou seest how few be the things, the which if
a man has at his command his life flows gently on
and is divine.
—*Marcus Aurelius*

THE HUSBAND

For him she plays, to him she sings
  Of early faith and plighted vows;
  She knows but matters of the house,
And he—he knows a thousand things.
—*Alfred Tennyson*

[75]

GOOD FELLOWS

The peer I don't envy, I'll give him his bow;
I scorn not the peasant, though ever so low;
But a club of good fellows, like those that are here
And a bottle like this, are my glory and cheer.
　　　　　　　　　　—*Robert Burns*

WOMAN

Woman is the masterpiece.
                    —*Confucius*

Men have sight, women insight.
                    —*Hugo*

O fairest of creation, last and best!
                    —*Milton*

Who is it can read a woman?
                    —*Shakespeare*

Ah, Mr. President, woman is a mystery. It has been well said that woman is the great conundrum of the nineteenth century; but if we cannot guess her, we will never give her up.
                    —*General Horace Porter*

Woman is the Sunday of man; not his repose only, but his joy; the salt of his life.
                    —*Michelet*

Without woman, man would be rough, rude, solitary, and would ignore all the graces, which are but the smiles of love.
                    —*Chateaubriand*

Every woman is wrong until she cries, and then she is right, instantly.
                    —*Haliburton*

All women are, in some degree, poets in imagination, angels in heart, and diplomatists in mind.
                    —*Emanuel Gonzales*

The Human Family

When Eve brought woe to all mankind
  Old Adam called her woe man,
But when she woo'd with love so kind
  He then pronounced her woman.

But now, with folly and with pride,
  Their husbands' pockets trimming,
The ladies are so full of whims
  That people call them w(h)imen.
—Anon.

With all women, gentleness is the most persuasive and powerful argument.
—Théophile Gauthier

Women like brave men exceedingly, but audacious men still more.
—Lemesles

They say women and music should never be dated.
—Goldsmith

Women have more strength in their looks than we have in our laws, and more power by their tears than we have by our arguments.
—Saville

When women love us, they forgive everything, even our crimes; when they do not love us, they do not credit even our virtues.
--Balzac

[78]

A beautiful woman is . . . the paradise of the eyes.
—*Fontenelle*

What is woman? One of Nature's agreeable blunders.
—*Cowley*

A woman's hopes are woven of sunbeams; a shadow annihilates them.
—*George Eliot*

Next to God we are indebted to woman, first for life itself, and then for making it worth living.
—*Bovée*

To describe women, the pen should be dipped in the humid colors of the rainbow, and the paper dried with the dust gathered from the wings of a butterfly.
—*Diderot*

Earth's noblest thing,—a woman perfected.
—*Lowell*

She is a woman, therefore may be woo'd;
She is a woman, therefore may be won.
—*Shakespeare*

What will not woman, gentle woman, dare,
When strong affection stirs her spirit up!
—*Southey*

A child of our Grandmother Eve, a female;
Or, for thy more sweet understanding, a woman.
—*Shakespeare*

O woman! in our hours of ease
Uncertain, coy, and hard to please,
And variable as the shade
By the light quivering aspen made;
When pain and anguish wring the brow,
A ministering angel thou!
—*Scott*

Woman is woman's natural ally.
—*Euripides*

O woman! lovely woman! Nature made thee
To temper man: we had been brutes without you.
Angels are painted fair, to look like you:
There's in you all that we believe of heaven,—
Amazing brightness, purity and truth,
Eternal joy and everlasting love.
—*Otway*

There's a woman like a dewdrop, she's so purer
than the purest.
—*Browning*

'Tis woman that seduces all mankind;
By her we first were taught the wheedling arts.
—*Gay*

Woman has this in common with angels, that
suffering beings belong especially to her.
—*Balzac*

A woman who has successfully cultivated her mind without diminishing the gentleness and propriety of her manners, is always sure to meet with a respect and attention bordering upon enthusiasm.

—Sidney Smith

There is a secret drawer in every woman's heart.

—Hugo

There was never yet a fair woman, but she made mouths in the glass.

—Shakespeare

Woman is a spirituality between man and the angels.

—Balzac

When a woman pronounces the name of a man but twice in a day, there may be some doubts as to the nature of her sentiments; but three times!

—Balzac

The perfect woman is as beautiful as she is strong, as tender as she is sensible. She is calm, deliberate, dignified, leisurely. She is gay, graceful, sprightly, sympathetic. She is severe upon occasion and upon occasion playful. She has fancies, dreams, romances, ideas.

—Gail Hamilton

Woman once made equal to man becomes his superior.

—Socrates

FATHERS AND MOTHERS

" Honor thy father and thy mother " stands written among the three laws of most revered righteousness.

—*Aeschylus, 524-456 B.C.*

This expression of ours: "Father of a family."
—*Pliny the Younger, 61-105 A.D.*

A mother is a mother still—
The holiest thing alive.

—*Coleridge*

Oh, when a mother meets on high
The babe she lost in infancy,
Hath she not then for pains and fears,
The day of woe, the watchful night,
For all her sorrow, all her tears,
An over-payment of delight ?

—*Southey*

Here's to Mothers; the guide-posts to Heaven.
—*Meusa*

SWEETHEARTS AND WIVES

Our dreams and inspirations, our ambitions, balance-wheels and financiers, guides and comforts, counsellors and comrades.

—*Pseud.*

Some sing of the ruby wine
Or the humming home-brewed ale.
Some glory in tavern toasts
With comrades hearty and hale.
But give me a forest health,
The blue sky roof above;
I drain this glass to the bonny lass,
The lass of my own true love.

Then here's to the maid ye love, my lads,
And here's to her promise true.
And here's to the blue of the sky in her eye
And the print of her tiny shoe.
I drink to her sunny hair, my lads.
I drink to her lips rose red.
The lass you love is the world to you
When all's been done and said.
                    —*Robert Emmet Mac Alarney,*
                        In "Ye Mayde of Yorke."

The bubbles rise less joyously
    To sparkling brim, in ready mirth,
Than to our lips this health; as we
    Drink to the sweetest toast on earth.
                    —*Robert G. Anderson*

A wife full of truth, innocence and love is the
prettiest flower that a man can wear next to his
heart.
                    —*Childs*

[83]

HUSBANDS

A good husband makes a good wife.

—Farquhar

The husband is the shrine for woman's love; a woman's staff and woman's shield, the architect of home.

—Annie E. Lancaster

A master of a house, as I have read,
Must be the first man up, and the last in bed.
—Robert Herrick

WIVES

Love thy wife as thyself; honor her more than thyself.

—Rabbi Simon

A good wife is a fortune to a man, especially if she is poor.

—Michelet

Men do not know their wives well; but wives know their husbands perfectly.

—Feuillet

BOYS AND GIRLS

Love is a boy by poets styl'd;
Then spare the rod and spoil the child.
—Samuel Butler

Queen rose of the rosebud garden of girls
—Tennyson

Boys are boys, and not little men; they all in- ***The***
herit the same pride, the same ambition, the same ***Human***
spirit of mischief, and the same freemasonry of
mutual confidence in all affairs relating to the ***Family***
governing of the boy-world.
—*Shirley Hibbard*

A boy has a natural genius for combining business with pleasure.
—*Charles Dudley Warner*

All girls are good. . . .
—*Minot*

Girls were created to love and be loved.
—*Ceri*

Girls we love for what they are; young men for
what they promise to be.
—*Goethe*

Auld Nature swears the lovely dears
Her noblest work she classes, O;
Her prentice han' she tried on man,
And then she made the lasses, O!
— *Burns*

Princes, to you the Western breeze
Bears many a ship and heavy laden,
What is the best we send in these?
A free and frank young Yankee maiden.
—*Brander Matthews*

Oh would I were a boy again,
When life seemed formed of sunny years,
And all the heart then knew of pain
Was wept away in transient tears!
—*Mark Lemon*

A school boy's tale, the wonder of an hour!
Ah, happy years! Once more who would not be
a boy?
—*Byron*

Like little wanton boys that swim on bladders.
—*Shakespeare*

Golden lads and girls all must
As chimney-sweepers come to dust.
—*Shakespeare*

GIRL GRADUATES

Love and thought and fun are free.
All must flirt in their degree.
Books alone have never reared
Sweet girl-graduates, golden haired.
—*W. E. Henley*

BABIES

Babies are the fragile beginnings of a mighty
end.　　　　　　　　—*Caroline E. Norton*

A babe in a house is a well-spring of pleasure, a
messenger of peace and love.
—*Tupper*

[86]

A babe's breast against a mother's bosom fans
the holiest flame that ever kindles the heart.
—Tupper

> Hush! my dear, lie still and slumber;
>   Holy angels guard thy bed!
> Heavenly blessings without number
>   Gently falling on thy head.
> —Watts,
"Cradle Hymn."

An infant—a sweet new blossom of humanity,
fresh fallen from God's own home to flower on
earth.
—Gerald Massey

> A mother's pride, a father's joy.
> —Scott

The Babies: As they comfort us in our sorrows,
let us not forget them in our festivities.
—Mark Twain
(Quotation from a speech at a banquet given by the
Army of the Tennessee at Chicago, Ill., November 13,
1879.)

CHILD

The child is father of the man.
—Wordsworth

A child is a man in a small letter.
—Bishop Earle

A child is an angel dependent on man.

—*Maistre*

A child's existence is a bright, soft element of joy.

—*George B. Rodney*

SCHOOLMASTERS

The cares of a schoolmaster are as heavy as those of a king.

—*Dionysius*

The schoolmaster's chair is the throne of a republican government.

—*Tunis G. Bergen, Jr.*

A good schoolmaster is worth to a town more than the best house, the best farm, or the most valuable estate in it.

—*Theodore Dwight. Jr.*

TRIBUTE TO HUMANITY

I live for those who love me,
  For those who know me true,
For the heaven that bends above me,
  And the good that I can do;
For the wrongs that need resistance,
  For the cause that lacks assistance,
For the future in the distance
  And the good that I can do.

—*Thomas Guthrie*

Our Country

TRIBUTES

We join ourselves to no party that does not carry the flag and keep step to the music of the union.

—*Rufus Choate*

Let our object be our country, our whole country, and nothing but our country.

—*Daniel Webster*

The moment I heard of America, I loved her; the moment I heard she was fighting for freedom, I burnt with a desire of bleeding for her; and the moment I shall be able to serve her at any time, or in any part of the world, will be the happiest of my life.

—*Lafayette*

I once heard an Irishman say, "Every man loves his native land whether he was born there or not."

—*Thomas Fitch*

SAXON GRIT

Saxon grit is the story of a thousand years. It is the struggle of millions of men on battle fields in two worlds.

—*Rev. Robert Collyer*

Sail on, O ship of state!
Sail on, O union, strong and great!
Humanity, with all its fears,
With all the hopes of future years,
Is hanging breathless on thy fate!

Sail on, nor fear to breast the sea!
Our hearts, our hopes, are all with thee;
Our hearts, our hopes, our prayers, our tears,
Our faith triumphant o'er our fears,
Are all with thee—are all with thee!

—*Longfellow*

The proper means of increasing the love we bear to our native country is to reside some time in a foreign one.

—*Shenstone*

Our country! In her intercourse with foreign nations may she always be right; but our country right or wrong.

—*Stephen Decatur*

Liberty when it begins to take root is a plant of rapid growth.

—*Washington*

The English speaking race—the founders of **Our Country** commonwealths; pioneers of progress; stubborn defenders of liberty—may they ever work together for the world's welfare.

—*Charles Stewart Smith*

(Toast proposed by Mr. Smith, and responded to by George William Curtis, at the Chamber of Commerce Banquet, November 15th, 1887.)

America and England; and may they never have any division but the Atlantic between them.

—*Charles Dickens*

The day we celebrate—the second Birthday of New York. Out of the ashes of the Revolution in the gladsome light of Liberty and Peace, she rose to her place as the metropolis of the Continent.

—*George W. Lane*

(Toast proposed by Mr. Lane, and responded to by Joseph H. Choate, at the Chamber of Commerce Banquet, New York, November 26th, 1883.)

We do well to decorate alike the graves of Union and Confederate. Those who fought on the other side were doing their part equally well to settle the great question that had to be settled by the sword.

—*Walter Seth Logan*

SOLDIERS

The army is a school in which the niggardly become generous and the generous prodigal; and if there are some soldiers misers, they are a kind of monsters but very rarely seen.

—*Cervantes*

We soldiers drink, we soldiers sing,
We fight our foes, and love our king,
While all our wealth two words impart,
A knapsack and a cheerful heart.

—*Anon.*

Up! for the bugles are calling,
    Saddle, to boot, and away!
Sabres are clanking, and lances are glancing,
The colonel is swearing and horses are prancing,
    So up with the sabres and lances,
        Up and away!

—*William Sharp*

Come, Somersets, fill up your glasses,
    And drain them as dry as you can;
For luck to sweet Somerset lasses,
    And every stout Somerset man!

—*Anon.*

A soldier, a soldier, a soldier for me—
    His arms are so bright,
    And he looks so upright,
    So gallant and gay
    When he trips it away,
Who is so nice and well powder'd as he?
Sing rub a dub rub; a dub rub a dub; a dub a dub
  dub dub;
    Thunder and plunder!
A soldier, a soldier, a soldier for me!
                —*Anon.*

Then drink and sing,
    My brother soldiers bold,
To country and to king,
    Like jolly hearts of gold!
                —*Anon.*

We soldiers drink, we soldiers sing,
We fight our foes, and love our king,
    Are ever brisk and jolly;
We know no care, in peace or war,
We ask no wealth but fame and health,
    A knapsack and a Dolly.
                —*Anon.*

Soldiers are martyrs to ambition.
           —*Thomas B. Shaw*

[93]

Our Country

A soldier's vow to his country is, that he will die for the guardianship of her domestic virtue; of her righteous laws, and of her in any way challenged or endangered honor.

—Ruskin

For smiling lasses, brimming glasses,
Greet us home when daylight passes;
And then we sing to the skies above
A soldier's life is the life we love!
—N. J. Sporle

The heroes of all ages and of every land and
  clime
Have been sung in each and every kind of metre.
But I will sing the praises of a bonny fighting lad,
The bravest lad that ever smelled saltpetre.
He's just a faded flannel shirt, a dingy campaign
  hat,
A pair of torn and timeworn khaki trousers,
The rest of him is muscle, eagle eye and lion heart,
That keep him steady 'mong the cracking Mausers.
—Robert Emmet Mac Alarney,
in "The Little Jade Joss"

The drum is his pleasure, his joy and delight,
It leads him to feel pleasure as well as to fight;
There's never a girl, though ever so glum,
But packs up her tatters and follows the drum.
—John O'Keeffe

Boot, boot into the stirrup, lads,
  And hand once more on rein;
Up, up into the saddle, lads,
  Afield we ride again!
One cheer, one cheer for dame or dear,
  No leisure now to sigh,
God bless them all—we have their prayers,
  And they our hearts—"good-bye!"
                    —*William Motherwell*

Up, up, and arm thee, son of terror,
Be thy bright shield the morning's mirror!
                    —*Sir Walter Scott*

SAILORS
Sailors are almost all believers.
                    —*R. H. Dana, Jr.*

The life of a tar is the life I love;
The sea is beneath us, the heavens above:
Our reign undisputed from the sky to the sea,
Whose life can compare to the mariner free?
                    —*Anon*

A sailor's life's a life for me,
He takes his duty merrily;
If winds can whistle, he can sing,
Still faithful to his friend and king;
He gets beloved by all the ship,
And toasts his girl and drinks his flip.
                    —*Charles Dibdin*

The experience of all nations proves that the
navy is the best defence of a country.
                    —*Timothy Dwight*

Our Country

Jack dances and sings, and is always content,
  In his vows to his lass he'll ne'er fail her.
His anchor's a-trip when his money's all spent—
  And this is the life of a sailor.
                    —*Charles Dibdin*

Away with bayonet and with lance,
  With corselet, casque and sword;
Our island-king no war-horse needs,
  For on the sea he's lord.
His throne's the warship's lofty deck,
  His sceptre is the mast;
His kingdom is the rolling wave,
  His servant is the blast.
                    —*Thomas Dibdin*

The sailor considers it but in line of duty to risk his life for the defence of his country.
                    —*Marryat*

There is much in the character of the sailor which leads us to make allowance for his irregularities; his frankness, his good nature, his courage, his attachment to his country, all enlist us in his favor.
                    —*George Mogridge (Old Humphrey)*

A seaman's life is a life I love,
  And one I'll live and die,
With the sea below and sky above,
  And the billows mountains high.
                    —*Anon.*

PATRIOTS

Such is the patriot's boast where'er we roam,
His first, best country ever is his own.

—*Goldsmith*

To scatter plenty o'er a smiling land
And read their history in a nation's eyes.

—*Gray's Elegy*

When our country's cause provokes to arms,
How martial music every bosom warms!

—*Pope*

   To fight,
In a just cause, and for our country's glory,
Is the best office of the best of men;
And to decline when these motives urge,
Is infamy beneath a coward's baseness.

—*Havard's Regulus*

The whole world will honor the statesman who
lifts from it the intolerable burden of war.

—*J. G. Whittier*

Patriots in peace assert the people's right,
With noble stubbornness resisting might.

—*Dryden*

This nation, under God, shall have a new birth
of freedom, and that government of the people, by
the people, for the people, shall not perish from the
earth.

—*Lincoln*

Our Country

I only regret that I have but one life to lose for my country.

—*Nathan Hale*

O Liberty! can man resign thee!
Once having felt thy generous flame?
Can dungeon, bolts, and bars confine thee,
Or whip thy noble spirit tame?

—*Rouget de Lisle*

OUR FLAG

One flag, one land, one heart, one hand, one nation evermore.

—*Anon.*

The Flag—the old Flag! At last it waves upon the soil of every State. It flaunts defiance in the face of treason, and soon shall float in triumph and honor over the unhallowed grave.

—*Henry A. Hurlburt*
(*Toast responded to by Major General John A. Dix at the 85th Annual Dinner of the New England Society in New York, December 22d, 1863.*)

Nail to the mast our holy flag,
Set every threadbare sail,
And give to the god of storms,
The lightning and the gale.

—*Oliver Wendell Holmes*

If any one attempts to haul down the American flag, shoot him on the spot.

—*John A. Dix*

[98]

O folds of white and scarlet! O blue field with **Our Country** your silver stars! May fond eyes welcome you, willing feet follow you, strong hands defend you, warm hearts cherish you, and dying lips give you their blessing! Ours by inheritance, ours by allegiance, ours by affection,—long may you float on the free winds of heaven, the emblem of liberty, the hope of the world!

—*Anon.*

A star for every State, a State for every star.
—*Robert C. Winthrop*

Then up with our flag!—let it stream on the air;
Though our fathers are cold in their graves,
They had hands that could strike, they had souls
    that could dare,
And their sons were not born to be slaves.
Up, up with that banner! Where'er it may call,
Our millions shall rally around,
And a nation of free men that moment shall fall
When its stars shall be trailed on the ground.
—*George Washington Cutter*

Look! Americans, look! Look up to the sky!
Don't you see it waving there, far, far up on high?
See! See! The Flag of Freedom! The Flag of
    the True!
Look! Patriots! 'Tis the glorious red, white, and
    blue.
—*George F. Taylor*

UNCLE SAM

Here's to Uncle Sam: the most respected, genial,
farcical, picturesque, courteous, gallant, hospitable,
generous, liberty-loving, calm, judicial, honorable,
misunderstood old myth that ever was invented.

—*Pseud.*

THE AMERICAN EAGLE

Majestic monarch of the cloud!
Who rear'st aloft thy regal form,
To hear the tempest trumping loud,
And see the lightning lances driven,
When strive the warriors of the storm,
And rolls the thunder drum of heaven!
Child of the sun! to thee 'tis given
To guard the banner of the free,
To hover in the sulphur smoke,
To ward away the battle-stroke,
And bid its blindings shine afar,
Like rainbows in a cloud of war—
The harbingers of victory.

—*Anon.*

OUR PRESIDENTS

Here's to past presidents, the present president,
and coming presidents. Some, long on praise and
short on blame; some, short on praise and long
on blame; but all long on votes. May they be
immortalized in our family portraits and in the
"Lives of the Presidents."

—*Pseud*

OUR YANKEE GIRLS

Our own sweet Yankee girls!
Our free-born Yankee girls!
God bless our Yankee girls!
　　　　—*Oliver Wendell Holmes*

THE UNITED STATES

We who are native born have a country of
which we may well be proud. Those of us who
have been abroad are better able, perhaps, to make
the comparison of our enjoyments and our comforts
than those who have stayed at home.
　　　　—*Ulysses S. Grant*

(*Quotation from the toast, "The United States, the
Greatest Modern Republic," proposed by George W.
Lane and responded to by General Grant at the Annual
Banquet of the Chamber of Commerce, May 8th, 1883.*)

Nature

TRIBUTES

Art imitates Nature.

—*Richard Franck, 1658*

Let Nature be your teacher.

—*Wordsworth*

Everything in Nature contains all the powers of
Nature.   Everything is made of one hidden stuff.

—*Emerson*

Nature teaches beasts to know their friends.

—*Shakespeare*

Recognizes ever and anon
The breezes of Nature stirring in his soul.

—*Wordsworth*

To him, who in the love of Nature holds com-
munion with her visible forms, she speaks a various
language.   Go forth under Nature's sky, and list
to Nature's teachings.

—*Bryant*

I trust in Nature for the stable laws of beauty 𝕹ature
and utility.   Spring shall plant and Autumn garner
to the end of time.

—Browning

THE OCEAN

The ocean is the navigator's world.

—William Baffin

There is something magnificent and imposing in
the changelessness of the ocean.

—Lady Blessington

How numberless are the blessings we owe to the
ocean, the father and sustainer of all organic life.

—George Hartwig

The ocean is the throbbing heart of the universe.

—Miss C. Talbott.

The surgy murmurs of the lonely sea.

—Keats

The Sea! the Sea! the open Sea!
The blue, the fresh, the ever free!
Without a mark, without a bound,
It runneth the earth's wide regions 'round;
It plays with the clouds; it mocks the skies;
Or like a cradled creature lies.

—Barry Cornwall

Nature

The sea is open to all.

—*Zarco*

The sea is the voyager's home.
—*Sir John Chardin*

The sea is the heaving bosom of the world.
—*Fell*

The sea is the world's depot for lost and unreclaimed baggage.
—*Nathaniel Lardner*

What a wonder is the sea! How wide it stretches out its arms, clasping islands and continents in its embrace! How mysterious are its depths; still more mysterious its hoarded and hidden treasures!
—*John Pierpont*

This sea that bares her bosom to the moon.
—*Wordsworth*

The Ocean, with its vastness, its blue green,
Its ships, its rocks, its caves, its hopes, its fears—
Its voice mysterious, which whoso hears
Must think on what will be, and what has been.
—*Keats*

And white waves heaving high, my boys,
   The good ship tight and free—
The world of waters is our home,
   And merry men are we.
               —Allan Cunningham

The timbers creak, the sea-birds shriek,
   There's lightning in the blast!
Hard to the leeward, mariners,
   For the storm is gathering fast.
               —Anon.

THE EARTH

The earth is our mother.
               —Junius Brutus

The earth is a piece of divine architecture.
               —T. Burnet

If you tickle the earth with a hoe she laughs
with a harvest.
               —Douglas Jerrold

The earth yields us blessings every year, and
friendship every moment.
               —Demophilus

RAIN

How beautiful is the rain.
               —Longfellow

Rain may fall as gently as mercy.
—*Richard Grant White*

As tears soften the heart, so does rain soften the earth, that good may come.
—*Annie E. Lancaster*

In the truest sense of the word, rain deserves to be called a present from heaven.
—*Sturm*

TREES

Cause not a tree to die.
—*King of Siam*

Plant and protect good trees
—*William Forsyth*

A tree is the gift of heaven to man.
—*Yu-ta*

Trees shade us, but they know it not.
—*Ben Jonson*

He who plants trees loves others besides himself.
—*Sir Hans Sloane*

THE WOODS

Woods are the abode of Deity.
—*Hualcop*

How sweet is the quiet of friendly woods, free from the cares and anxieties of city life!
—*Penn*

In the woods a man casts off his years as the snake his slough, and at what period soever of life is always a child; in the woods is perpetual youth; in the woods we return to reason and faith.

—*Emerson*

ROCKS

Rocks show the lapse of ages.
—*James Dwight Dana*

The sea ebbs and flows, but the rock remains firm.
—*Rutherford*

Rocks constitute the solid basis and principal bulk of the globe.
—*Sir Charles Lyell*

SCENERY

Nature affords plenty of beautiful scenes, that no man need complain.
—*Rymer*

Purer pleasure I have never felt than in gazing upon the wild scenery of nature, in all her grandeur and beauty.
—*Audubon*

To contemplate scenery exerts a highly purifying, elevating and even religious influence over the mind, and weans vice from virtue.
—*Orson Squire Fowler*

MOUNTAINS

Mountains are the bulwarks of nature, to shelter countries against the furies of the seas and storms, and, like ramparts and natural fortifications, they protect several states from the invasion of enemies and the ambition of conquerors.

—Sturm

Mountains have a grand, stupid, lovable tranquillity.

—Oliver Wendell Holmes

THE PRAIRIE

The prairie is primeval nature.

—Chadbourne

There is an air of refinement on a prairie that wins the heart.

—James Hall

The prairies are the gardens of the desert, the unshorn fields, boundless and beautiful.

—Bryant

THE RIVER

A River is a public highway.

—John Barr

Rivers bless mankind; Egypt itself is the gift of the Nile.

—Herodotus

A full and clear river is, in my opinion, the most poetical object in nature.

—*Sir Humphrey Davy*

The beginnings of a river are insignificant, and its infancy is frivolous; it plays among the flowers of a meadow; it waters a garden, or turns a little mill. Gathering strength in its youth, it becomes wild and impetuous; increased by numerous alliances, and advanced in its course, it becomes grave and stately in its motions, and in majestic silence rolls on its mighty waters till it is laid to rest in the vast abyss.

—*Pliny*

Nature's Jewels

FLOWERS

Flowers are Nature's jewels.

—*G. Croly*

The flowers in silence seem to breathe
Such thoughts as language could not tell.

—*Byron*

The violet droops its soft and bashful brow,
But from its heart sweet incense fills the air,—
So rich within—so pure without—art thou,
With modest mien and so·l of virtue rare.

—*Anon.*

Here are sweet-peas, on tiptoe for a flight:
With wings of gentle flush o'er delicate white,
And taper fingers catching at all things,
To bind them all about with tiny rings.

—*John Keats*

And in that golden vase was set
The prize—the golden violet.
—The Troubadour

    Go, lovely rose!
Tell her that wastes her time and me
    That now she knows,
When I resemble her to thee,
How sweet and fair she seems to be.
—Waller

The rose is fairest when 'tis budding new,
    And hope is brightest when it dawns from fears.
The rose is sweetest wash'd with morning dew,
    And love is loveliest when embalmed in tears.
—Scott

A rose is sweeter in the budde than full blowne.
—Lyly, 1553-1601

There's rosemary, that's for remembrance.
—Shakespeare

    Sweet rose! thy crimson leaves
    Are little happy thieves!
—Edwin Arnold

Myriads of daisies have shone forth in flower
Near the lark's nest, and in their natural hour
Have passed away; less happy than the one
That, by the unwilling ploughshare, died to prove
The tender charm of poetry and love.
—Wordsworth

Nature's Jewels

Under a lawn, than skies more clear,
Some ruffled roses nestling were:
And, snuggling there, they seem'd to lie
As in a flowery nunnery.
                    —*Robert Herrick*

There is pansies, that's for thoughts.
                    —*Shakespeare*

Like the sweet sound, that breathes upon a bank
    of violets.
                    —*Twelfth Night*

The rose is a token of joy and love.
                    —*Percival*

FRUIT

Fruits enhance an inheritance.
                    —*Bouvier*

The fruit tree is an emblem of life; culture
improves its beauty and usefulness.
                    —*Drelincourt*

Doubtless God could have made a better fruit
than the strawberry, but God never did.
                    —*Botiler*

Joys and Blessings

WORK

Work done may claim its wages.

—*Tupper*

Work is the best thing to make us love life.

—*Ernest Renan*

There is a perennial nobleness and even sacredness in work; were he never so benighted, forgetful of his calling, there is always hope in a man that actually and earnestly works; in idleness alone there is perpetual despair.

—*Carlyle*

Sleep hovers with extended wing
Above the roof where labor dwells.

—*Horace*

LABOR

Labor conquers all things.

—Virgil

Labor, even, is pleasant at all times.

—Euripides

Labor has a bitter root, but a sweet taste.

—Halm

POETS

The poets are the finest interpreters of life.

—David G. Downey

A poet heeds not the reverse of fortune.

—Camoens

True poets are lovers of the poor; they are knight
errants of the downtrodden.

—Theodore Tilton

Poets view nature as a book in which they
read language unknown to common minds, as
astronomers read the heavens and therein discover
objects that escape the vulgar ken.

—John Angill James

The bards may go down to the place of their slum-
bers;
The lyre of the charmer be hushed in the grave;
But far in the future the power of their numbers
Shall kindle the hearts of our faithful and brave.

—Frances Brown

POETRY

Poetry is the eloquence of truth.

—Campbell

Poetry is the morning dream of great minds.
—Lamartine

Poetry is the reward of the best and happiest moments of the happiest and best minds.

—Shelley

Poetry is the utterance of truth—deep heartfelt truth; the true poet is very near the oracle.
—Edwin Hubbell Chapin

Sculpture and painting are moments of life; poetry is life itself and everything around it, and above it.

—Walter Savage Landor

AUTHORS

An author departs; he does not die.
—Miss Mulock

Authors are the glory of the world.

—Delrio

Authors are the doctors of the laws.

—Henry I

Authors, like corns, grow dearer as they grow older.

—Pope

[115]

Let others glut on the extorted praise
Of vulgar breath; trust thou to after-days:
Thy labor'd works shall live, when Time devours
Th' abortive offspring of their hasty hours.

—*Thomas Carew*

BOOKS

A book is the only immortality.

—*Rufus Choate.*

Books are embalmed minds.

—*Bovée*

Books make up no small part of human happiness.

—*Frederick the Great*

A book is a friend that never deceives.

—*Pixérécourt*

Next to acquiring good friends the best acquisition is that of good books.

—*Colton*

As good almost kill a man as kill a good book; who kills a man, kills a reasonable creature, God's image; but he who destroys a good book, kills reason itself.

—*Milton*

And books, we know,
Are a substantial world both pure and good:
Round these, with tendrils strong as flesh and blood,
Our pastime and our happiness will grow.

—*Anon.*

Go, little book, and wish to all
Flowers in the garden, meat in the hall,
A bin of wine, a spice of wit,
A house with lawns enclosing it,
A living river by the door,
A nightingale in the sycamore!
                    —*Robert Louis Stevenson*
                        in "Poems and Ballads,"
                    pub. by Charles Scribner's Sons

Joys and Blessings

'Twas goodly fame, once on a time,
To write a book of prose or rhyme.
But years upset the scheme of things.
No book, to author, honor brings,
Unless five ciphers tell the tale—
(Supremest test!) A ready sale.
                    —*Stanlicus*

There is no frigate like a book
    To take us leagues away,
Nor any coursers like a page
    Of prancing poetry.
This traverse may the poorest take
    Without oppress or toll;
How frugal is the chariot
    That bears the human soul!
                    —*Emily Dickinson*
        (*Kind permission of Little, Brown & Co.*)

These books upon their shelf...remind me of my
other self, younger and stronger, and the pleasant
ways in which I walked.
                    —*Longfellow*

[117]

Joys and Blessings

These are my books—a Burton old,
A Lamb arrayed against the cold;
    In polished dress of red and blue,
    A rare old Elzevir or two,
And Johnson, clothed in green and gold.

A Pope, in gilded calf, I sold
To buy a Sterne, of worth untold,
    To cry, as bibliomaniacs do,
        "These are my books!"

What though a Fate unkind hath doled
But favors few to me, yet bold
    My little wealth abroad I strew
    To purchase acquisitions new,
And say, by love of them controlled,
        "These are my books!"
                        —*Nathan M. Levy*

Each life of man is but a page
In God's great diary; each age
A separate volume and each race
A chapter. For a little space
We write, and childlike, cry our powers,
Nor deem His hand is guiding ours.
                        —*Post Wheeler*

THE BOOKWORMS

Through and through the inspired leaves,
Ye maggots make your windings;
But, oh, respect his lordship's taste,
And spare the golden bindings!
                        —*Burns*

To turn my volumes o'er nor find
  Sweet unsuspicious friend;
Some vestige of an erring mind
  To chide or discommend,
Believe that all were lov'd like you
  With love from blame exempt,
Believe that all my griefs were true
  And all my joys but dreamt.
          —*Walter Savage Landor*

LIBRARY

A good library is a great kingdom.
          —*Magliabecchi*

My library is a friend of a thousand years.
          —*Kyo-Sya*

Within the sacred walls of libraries we find the
best thoughts, the purest feelings, and the most
exalted imagings of our race.
          —*Bovée*

READING

Read good books.
          —*John Todd*

Reading enriches the memory.
          —*Jeissier*

Reading is the perfection of pleasure.
          —*Magliabecchi*

To read without reflecting is like eating without digesting.

—*Burke*

No entertainment is so cheap as reading, nor any pleasure so lasting.

—*Lady Montague*

LITERATURE

Literature is the tongue of the world.

—*Thomas Paine*

Literature is the immortality of speech.

—*R. A. Willmott*

Literature is an avenue to glory, ever open for those ingenious men who are deprived of honors and of wealth.

—*William Hornberg*

FICTION

Fiction hath in it a higher end than fact.

—*Anon.*

Those who delight in the study of human nature may improve in the knowledge of it, and in the profitable application of that knowledge by the perusal of fiction.

—*Richard Whately*

Fiction is Poetry's big brother.

—*Pseud.*

Fiction is a boon to critics and dreary hours. **Joys** It opens up avenues of conversation, makes us **and** forget the long journey, the disappointing day, the **Blessings** rainy holiday, and inspires us with a zest to do things.

—Pseud.

And truth severe by fairy fiction drest.

—Thomas Gray

We know to tell many fictions like to truths, and we know, when we will, to speak what is true.

—Hesiod
Circa 720 B.C.

PRINTING

Printing is the materialization of thought.

—Day

Printing unfolds the thoughts of man and immortalizes them.   —Anon.

The invention of printing added a new element of power to the race; from that hour, in a most especial sense, the brain and not the arm, the thinker and not the soldier, books and not kings, were to rule the world.

—Edwin Percy Whipple

ARCHITECTURE

Architecture is frozen music.

—Mme. de Staël

Architecture exhibits the greatest extent of the difference from nature which may exist in works of art; it involves all the powers of design, and shows the greatness of man and should teach him humility.

—Coleridge

ART

Art is nature concentrated.

—Balzac

Art helps nature, and experience art.

—Rembrandt

Art is mighty; for art is the work of man under the guidance and inspiration of a mightier power than man.

—J. C. Hare

Art, as far as it has the ability, follows nature, as a pupil imitates his master; thus your art must be, as it were, God's grandchild.

—Dante

THE ARTIST

Artists are men of subtle craft.

—John Galt

An artist has more than two eyes.

—Haliburton

MUSIC

Music is the harmony of the soul.

—Swinburne

Music is the highest of all sciences.

—*Bach*

Music is a harbinger of eternal melody.

—*Mozart*

Music washes away from the soul the dust of
every-day life.

—*Auerbach*

Music is the mediator between the spiritual
and the sensual life.

—*Beethoven*

Music once admitted to the soul becomes a sort
of spirit, and never dies; it wanders perturbedly
through the halls and galleries of the memory,
and is often heard again, distinct and living as when
it first displaced the wavelets of the air.

—*Bulwer*

Begin to charm, and, as thou strok'st mine ears
With thy enchantment, melt me into tears.
Then let thy active hand scud o'er the lyre,
And make my spirits frantic with the fire.
That done, sink down into a silvery strain,
And make me smooth as balm and oil again.

—*Robert Herrick*

SONG

Song is the tone of feeling.

—*J. C. Hare*

Angels were the first beings to sing songs.

—*John Gill*

[123]

A song will outlive all sermons in the memory.
—Henry Giles

Song brings of itself a cheerfulness that wakes the heart to joy.

—Euripides

CULTURE

Culture expands the reason.
—Caroline Bauer

Culture of the mind is the gift of luxury.
—Lynch

Cultivation of the mind is as necessary as food to the body.

—Cicero

SCULPTURE

Sculpture is a letter to posterity.
—Edward Parsons Day

Sculpture lives in lifeless marble.
—Bouchardon

Sculpture breaks the marble's sleep.
—Johan Tobias Sergel

Sculpture is the art of discarding superfluities.
—Antonio Canova

REST

On with thy work, though thou be'st hardly press'd:
Labor is held up by the hope of rest.

—Robert Herrick

THE EDITOR

Editors direct the current of thought.

—*Acton*

The editor lays every day a mass of facts before all people capable of thought.

—*Dickens*

The editor's work is allied to the stateman's, the politician's, and takes rank as it takes tribute of letters, science and law.

—*Manton Marble*

The editor of a newspaper is usually selected by his feeble-minded generation to bear the burden of their incapacity.

—*Horace Greeley*

REPORTERS

Reporters for the press have the advantage of gathering news from a thousand different persons, and from a thousand different things; the wise and the foolish, the learned and the ignorant, each in their turn furnish an item of news for the daily press.

—*James Ellis*

Reporters are ubiquitous.

—*Earl of Argyle*

Here's to reporters, the scapegoats of a busy age. They are called liars and bunco men. 'Tis in a measure true; but what of the givers of news??!!

—*Pseud.*

[125]

THE PRESS

News from the humming city comes to it.

—*Anon.*

The press is the royal seat on which knowledge
is sovereign.

—*J. H. Hammond*

The press reflects, leads and enforces the growth
of freedom and independence.

—*Samuel Bowles*

The press is the exclusive literature of the masses;
to the millions it is literature, church and college.

—*Wendell Phillips.*

The press is the steam engine of moral power,
which, directed by the spirit of the age, will eventually crush imposture, superstition, and tyranny.

—*Chatfield*

NEWSPAPERS

Newspapers are the world's mirrors.

—*James Ellis*

The newspaper is the map whereon are traced
out tendencies and destinies; the chart to direct
the traveller and the settler to safe and pleasant
harborage.

—*Edmund Yates*

Of all those arts in which the wise excel,
Nature's chief masterpiece is writing well.

—*Anon.*

THE SUNDAY PAPER

The folio of four (400) pages happy work which not even critics criticise.

—With Apologies to Cowper

The Press—right or wrong; when right to be kept right; when wrong to be set right.

—Samuel D. Babcock

(Toast proposed by Mr. Babcock and responded to by Whitelaw Reid, at the 108th Annual Banquet of the Chamber of Commerce in New York, May 4th, 1876.)

JOURNALISM

Journalism is organized gossip.

—Edward Eggleston

Journalism has become prominent, if not pre-eminent, as a profession.

—C. F. Wingate

ADVERTISING

Advertising is not the road to success, but success itself.

—Albert D. Richardson

Advertise your business; I owe all my success to printer's ink.

—P. T. Barnum

The most truthful part of a newspaper is the advertisements.

—Thomas Jefferson

The man who pays more for shop rent than for advertising does not know his business.

—*Horace Greeley*

The advertisements which appear in a public journal take rank among the most significant indications of the state of society of that time and place.

—*Charles Dickens*

SCIENCE

Science unfolds the wisdom of God.

—*Juan de Pineda*

Science admires and bows to nature.

—*Strzelicki*

Science strengthens and enlarges the minds of men.

—*Lindley Murray*

Science is, I believe, nothing but trained, organized common sense.

—*Huxley*

PAINTING

Painting is silent poetry.

—*Simonides*

Painted pictures are dead speakers.

—*John Henry Fusili*

Painting is the intermediate something between thought and a thing.

—*Coleridge*

[128]

Town and Country

TOWN

If you would know and not be known, live in a city.

—*Colton*

Cities have always been the fireplaces of civilization, whence light and heat radiated out into the dark.

—*Theodore Parker*

The city is an epitome of the social world. All the belts of civilization intersect along its avenues; it contains the products of every moral zone; it is cosmopolitan not only in a national, but in a spiritual sense.

—*Alonzo B. Chapin*

COUNTRY

The country soothes us, refreshes us, lifts us up with religious reflections.

—*Edwin Hubbell Chapin*

The country is the philosopher's garden and library, in which he reads and contemplates the power, wisdom and goodness of God.

—*William Penn*

A country life gives a man a greater stock of health, and consequently a more perfect enjoyment of himself, than any other way of life.

—*Addison*

Amusements

ACTORS

An actor is a public instructor.

—*Euripides*

An actor refines public taste.

—*Anon.*

Actors are the only honest hypocrites.

—*Hazlitt*

THEATRE

The theatre is a mirror of life.

—*Sophocles*

The theatre is a chastener of vice.

—*Euripides*

The theatre is the devil's own territory.

—*Edward Allyn*

THE STAGE

The stage is a school of manners.

—*William Woodfall*

The stage represents fiction as if it were fact.

—*Betterton*

By the stage the people learn history.

—*Noevius*

The stage is the field for the orator as well as the comedian.

—*Roscius*

The stage is more powerful than the platform, the press or the pulpit.

—*Anna E. Dickinson*

THE DRAMA

The drama is a mirror of life.

—*John Liston*

The drama is the most refined pleasure of a polished people.

—*Dion Boucicault*

A passion for dramatic art is inherent in the nature of man.

—*Edwin Forrest*

It is in drama where poetry attains its loftiest flight.

—*Don Luis I. of Portugal*

The drama embraces and applies all the beauties **Amuse-** and decorations of poetry. The sister arts attend **ments** and adorn her; painting, architecture and music are her handmaidens; the costliest lights of a people's intellect burn at her show; all ages welcome her.

—Robert A. Willmott

When God conceived the world, that was Poetry; He formed it, and that was Scripture; He colored it, and that was Painting; He peopled it with living beings, and that was the grand, divine, eternal Drama.

—Charlotte Cushman

COMEDY

Death is jealous of a good comedy.

—Whitehead

A comedy is the wine-table of the mind.

—Taylor

A comedian is a genial public character.

—Shaw

A comedy is like a cigar: if good every one wants a box; if bad no amount of puffing will make it draw.

—Harry James Byron

Close to the Soil

IVY

The ivy teaches a lesson to man.
—*Mrs. Inchbald*

The ivy is the poet's image of constancy.
—*Archibald Geikie*

The ivy wreathing itself about an old and furrowed trunk is an emblem of devotion.
—*Hannah More*

SOIL

Improve the soil and the mind.
—*Colman*

He who owns the soil owns up to the sky.
—*Dallas*

Whatever is built on the soil belongs to the soil.
—*Pelletier*

THERE WAS A JOLLY MILLER

Close to the Soil

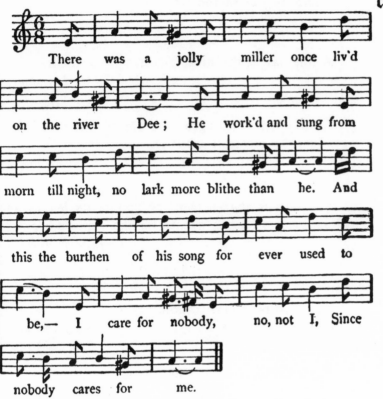

There was a jolly miller once liv'd on the river Dee; He work'd and sung from morn till night, no lark more blithe than he. And this the burthen of his song for ever used to be,— I care for nobody, no, not I, Since nobody cares for me.

I love my mill, she is to me like parent, child and wife;
I would not change my station for any other in life:
Then push, push, push the bowl, my boys, and pass it round to me;
The longer we sit here and drink, the merrier w shall be.

[135]

THE OAK

Venerate the sacred oak.

—*Druis*

A fine oak is the most picturesque of all trees.
—*J. C. Loudon*

A lofty oak is an agreeable object that invariably produces a pleasant emotion.

—*Kames*

The oak is the emblem of honor; its leaves are often used to form a wreath for the victor's brow.
—*James Ellis*

AGRICULTURE

Agriculture is civilization.

—*Emmons*

Agriculture is better than war.
—*Emperor Shun*

Agriculture is favorable to good morals.
—*Colman*

An agricultural life is one eminently calculated for human happiness and human virtue.
—*Josiah Quincy, Jr.*

HORTICULTURE

Horticulture is the true poetry of agriculture.
—*Theophilus Parsons*

The horticulturist is a lover of nature, and a true friend of art.
—*J. de la Quintinie*

Horticulture is a science in which are combined beauty, pleasure and profit.
—*Weidenmann*

FARMERS

I have fed like a farmer; I shall grow as fat as a porpoise.
—*Swift*

Good luck to the hoof and the horn!
Good luck to the flock and the fleece!
Good luck to the growers of corn!
With blessings of plenty and peace!
—*Anon.*

YORKSHIRE MINING TOAST

May all our labors be in vein.
—*Anon.*

TO THE LAND-OWNERS

Once upon a time there was a man who thought he wanted the earth. Then he had a vision, and he dreamed he did own the earth, and then he dreamed the assessor came around, and then he woke up.
—*George H. Daniels*

[137]

Close to the Soil

The farmer stands upon a lofty eminence, and looks upon the bustle of cities, the intricacies of mechanism, the din of commerce and brain-confusing, body-killing literature, with the feelings of personal freedom peculiarly his own.

—*L. C. Judson*

The farmers are the founders of civilization.

—*Daniel Webster*

RED CLOSE OF DAY.

A hundred flocks thy pastures roam:
Large herds, deep uddered, low around thy home
 At the red close of day;
 The steed with joyous neigh
Welcomes thy footstep.

—*Horace*

High Days and Holidays

FEAST DAYS

May our feast days be many and our fast days be few!

—*Mary L. Booth*

CHRISTMAS

Apple pie and Simon Beer,
Christmas comes but once a year.

—*Old Southern "Mammy" Saying*

The yearly course that brings this day about
Shall never see it but a holiday.

—*Shakespeare*

Forget not Christmas.

—*Henry IV. of England*

A regular orthodox jolly Christmas is suggestive of big fires, plum-puddings and family gatherings.

—*Alice Fisher*

[139]

Christmas is indeed the season of regenerated feeling—the season for kindling not merely the fire of hospitality in the hall, but the general flame of charity in the heart.

—Washington Irving

Old Christmas is come for to keep open house,
And scorn to be guilty of starving a mouse;
Then come, boys, and welcome, for diet the chief,
There's plum-pudding, roast goose, minced pies
     and roast beef.
Then let us be merry and taste the good cheer,
And remember old Christmas but comes once a year.

—Old Christmas Carol

I wish you a Merry Christmas
And a Happy New Year,
A pocket full of money,
And a cellar full of beer!

—Anon.

CHRISTMAS EVE

Come guard this night the Christmas-pie,
That the thief, though ne'er so sly,
With his flesh-hooks, don't come nigh
    To catch it.

—Robert Herrick

CANDLEMAS EVE

When yew is out, then birch comes in,
    And many flowers beside;
Both of a fresh and fragrant kin
    To honor Whitsuntide.

—Robert Herrick

[140]

CHRISTMAS TOAST

Drink now the strong beer;
Cut the white loaf here,
  The while the meat is a-shredding
For the rare mince-pie,
And the plums stand by
  To fill the paste that's a-kneading.

—*Robert Herrick*

ANOTHER CHRISTMAS TOAST

Come, help me to raise
Loud songs to the praise
Of good old English pleasures,
  To the Christmas cheer,
  And the foaming beer,
And the buttery's solid treasures;—

To the stout sirloin,
And the rich spiced wine,
And the boar's head grimly staring,
  To the frumenty,
  And the hot mince-pie
Which all folks were for sharing;—

To the holly and bay,
In their green array,
Spread over the walls and dishes;
  To the swinging sup
  Of the wassail cup,
With its toasted healths and wishes;—

[141]

To the honest bliss,
Of the hearty kiss,
Where the mistletoe was swinging,
When the berry white
Was claimed by right,
On the pale green branches clinging;—

To the story told
By the gossip old,
O'er the embers dimly glowing,
While the pattering sleet
On the casement beat
And the blast was hoarsely blowing;—

To all pleasant ways,
In those ancient days.
*   *   *   *   *

—*From A Fireside Book*

NEW YEAR'S DAY

Full knee-deep lies the winter snow,
And the winter winds are wearily sighing;
Toll ye the church bells sad and slow,
And tread softly and speak low,
For the old year lies a-dying.
...And let him in
That standeth here alone,
And waiteth at the door.
There's a new foot on the floor, my friend,
And a new face at the door, my friend,
A new face at the door.

—*Tennyson*

[142]

THANKSGIVING HYMN

The God of harvest praise;
In loud thanksgiving raise
   Hand, heart and voice.
The valleys laugh and sing,
Forests and mountains ring,
The plains their tribute bring,
   The streams rejoice.
        —*James Montgomery*

THANKSGIVING DAY

Thanksgiving Day! Thanksgiving Day!
'Tis then our nation tries to pay
Its heavy debt of gratitude
For bountiful supplies of food,
And richest blessings that expand
To cover all of Freedom's land.
        —*"Institute"*

FOURTH OF JULY

Let hoary dynasties forget
   Their natal story's fabling page;
Our country keeps her birthday yet
   And dares the world to doubt her age.
   *   *   *   *   *
Thy birthday and thy Washington's
   Are way-marks on the path of time;
Nor all the light of all thy suns
   Can dim the day-star of thy prime.
        —*Theron Brown,*
         in Harper's Bazar

WASHINGTON AND LINCOLN

Let none of us forget the Fourteenth and the Twenty-second of February of each year. There is room in our hearts for each of us to inspire a thoughtful, sincere, grateful and personal tribute to the memory of these fathers of our freedom.

—*Pseud.*

MEMORIAL DAY TRIBUTE

The nation that cherishes the graves of its soldiers and assembles to honor them is the nation that preserves and enlarges national life.

—*Benjamin Harrison*

ST. VALENTINE'S DAY

To-morrow is St. Valentine's day, all in the morning betime.

—*Hamlet*

THE MAY-POLE

The May-pole is up!
Now give me the cup,
I'll drink to the garlands around it;
But first unto those
Whose hands did compose
The glory of flowers that crown'd it.

—*Robert Herrick*

[144]

Seasons and Months

SEASONS

The seasons, like life, have four epochs.

—*Ovid*

The seasons have their own laws, and have their order arranged by heaven.

—*Seneca*

The peculiar charm of a country life in the society of nature consists in this: that we see the different seasons of the year roll past our eyes.

—*Humboldt*

SPRING

Wide flush the fields; the softening air is balm;
Echo the mountains round; the forest smiles;
And every sense and every heart is joy.

—*Thomson*

Seasons and Months

Now that the winter's gone, the earth has lost
Her snow white robes; and now no more the frost
Candies the grass, or casts an icy cream
Upon the silver lake or crystal stream.
       —Thomas Carew

When well-appareled April on the heels of limping Winter treads.
       —Shakespeare

Spring is the season of hope.
       —Lady Blessington

Spring is the boyhood of the year.
       —Tennyson

Spring is a beautiful piece of work.
       —N. P. Willis

Spring unlocks the flowers to paint the laughing soil.
       —Heber

Spring, the jovial, playful infancy of all living creatures, represents childhood and youth.
       —Stillingfleet

'Neath Spring's warm sighs
Hoar-headed Winter wakes, and dies:
Summer succeeds to vernal showers:
Autumn comes next with fruits and flowers.
The Winter lays his icy hand
Once more upon the sleeping land.
       —Horace

SUMMER

Summer is the sunshine of life.
—*José Francisco Isla*

Summer is the season when the Creator pours forth the treasures of His blessings in the greatest abundance.
—*Sturm*

AUTUMN

Autumn is the Sabbath of the year.
—*Logan*

Autumn, with its golden fruitage, waving fields, and gentle airs, its forests of variegated hue, its brown hill-sides regally clothed in purple, and its still waters slumbering in the drowsy sunshine, is exceedingly beautiful.
—*Charles J. Peterson*

AUTUMN

Then come the Autumne all in Yellow clad,
  As though he joyed in his plenteous store,
Laden with fruits that made him laugh full glad
  That he had banisht Hunger, which to fore
  Had by his belly oft him pinched sore;
Upon his Head a Wreath, that was enrolled
  With ears of Corne of every sort he bore,
And in his Hand a Sickle he did holde,
To reap the ripened Fruit the which the Earth
    had yold.
—*Spenser*

[147]

Autumn nodding o'er the yellow plain.

—*Thomson*

When Autumn lifts his comely head
With apple-wreath engarlanded,
What joy to pluck the grafted pear!
What pride the purple grapes to bear.

—*Horace*

WINTER

Winter is Nature's sleep.

—*H. S. Jacobs.*

There is a grandeur in winter, stern and wild
it may be, but a grandeur which speaks to the
soul.

—*C. J. Peterson*

Winter, so far from being prejudicial to the fruit-
fulness of the earth, is very favorable to it; this
is the season of rest so necessary to nature.

—*Sturm*

WINTER

Lastly came Winter, cloathed all in frize,
  Chattering his teeth for cold that did him chill;
Whilst on his hoary Beard his breath did freeze,
  And the dull drops that from his purple bill
  As from a limbeck did adown distill;
In his right hand a tipped staffe he held,
  With which his feeble steps he stayed still,
For he was faint with Cold and weak and eld,
That scarce his loosed limbes he able was to weld.

—*Spenser*

[148]

JANUARY

Lo, my fair! the morning lazy
  Peeps abroad from yonder hill;
Phœbus rises, red and hazy;
  Frost has stopped the village mill.

FEBRUARY

All around looks sad and dreary,
  Fast the flaky snow descends;
Yet the red-breast chirrups cheerly,
  While the mitten'd lass attends.

MARCH

Rise the winds and rocks the cottage,
  Thaws the roof, and wets the path;
Dorcas cooks the savory pottage;
  Smokes the cake upon the hearth.

APRIL

Sunshine intermits with ardor,
  Shades fly swiftly o'er the fields;
Showers revive the drooping verdure,
  Sweets the sunny upland yields.

MAY

Pearly beams the eye of morning;
  Child, forbear the deed unblest!
Hawthorn every hedge adorning,
  Pluck the flowers—but spare the nest.

[149]

JUNE

Schoolboys in the brook disporting,
  Spend the sultry hour of play;
While the nymphs and swains are courting,
  Seated on the new-mown hay.

JULY

Maids, with each a guardian lover,
  While the vivid lightning flies,
Hastening to the nearest cover,
  Clasp their hands before their eyes.

AUGUST

See the reapers, gleaning, dining,
  Seated on the shady grass;
O'er the gate the 'squire, reclining,
  Slily eyes each ruddy lass,

SEPTEMBER

Hark! a sound like distant thunder,
  Murderer, may thy malice fail!
Torn from all they love asunder,
  Widow'd birds around us wail.

OCTOBER

Now Pomona pours her treasure,
  Leaves autumnal strew the ground;
Plenty crowns the market measure,
  While the mill runs briskly round.

NOVEMBER

Now the giddy rites of Comus,
   Crown the hunter's dear delight;
Ah! the year is fleeing from us;
   Bleak the day, and drear the night.

DECEMBER

Bring more wood, and set the glasses,
   Join, my friends, our Christmas cheer,
Come, a catch!—and kiss the lasses—
   Christmas comes but once a year.
         —Hone's Year Book

MAY

Hail, bounteous May, that does inspire
Mirth, youth and warm desire:
Woods and groves are of thy dressing,
Hill and dale doth boast thy blessing.
         —Milton

JULY

First, April, she with mellow showers
Opens the way for early flowers;
Then after her comes smiling May,
In a more rich and sweet array;
Next enters June, and brings us more
Gems than those two that went before:
Then (lastly) July comes, and she
More wealth brings in than all those three.
         —Robert Herrick

𝔅irds and 𝔄nimals

BIRDS

Birds fill every grove with melody.
—*Albert Pickett*

The birds of the air are preachers of faith to man.
—*Luther*

The birds tell of heaven with their love-warblings in the green twilight.
—*Henry Ward Beecher*

The music of birds was the first song of thanksgiving which was offered on earth before man was formed.
—*George Horne*

That's the wise thrush; he sings each song twice over,
Lest you should think he never could recapture
The first fine careless rapture.
—*Browning*

BIRDS

In a small blue shell, the which a poor
Warm bird o'erspread, and sat still evermore,
Till her enclosed child kick'd, and pick'd itself a door.
—*John Donne*

EAGLE

The eagle has an empire in the air.
—*Jabir*

The eagle does not stoop to catch flies.
—*Florio*

The eagle is provided with pinions that outstrip
the wind.
—*G. W. Hervey*

O dainty duck!
—*Midsummer Night's Dream*

DOGS

Could we understand the language of animals,
how instructive would be a dialogue of dogs.
—*Eudoxus*

The dog is the only animal that leaves his own
species to take up his abode with man.
—*Goldsmith*

Dogs are one of the luxuries of civilization; in
uncivilized life they are perhaps more one of the
necessities.
—*Henry W. Shaw (Josh Billings)*

[153]

THE FOX

A fox is subtlety itself.

—Aristophanes

The fox counts hens in his dreams.

—Ismaeloff

THE HORSE

A man ought to do as well as a horse; I wish all men did as well.

—E. P. Roe

Men use care in purchasing a horse, and are neglectful in choosing friends.

—John Mair

A good horse is often man's best friend in time of danger.

—Israel Putnam

THE CAT

A little lion, small and dainty sweet,
With sea-green eyes and softly stepping feet.

—Anon.

THE COW—A BOVINITY

O, gentle cau,
Contented frau,
    Inert, exempt from violence.
We will allau
That you know hau
    To chew your cud in siolence.

—Pseud. Stanlicus

THE ACCUSING PARROT

O, disagreeable biped,
Be you green, or gray, or stripéd,
We would that you were wipéd
From our sight.

For when a man comes stealing
Up his steps, a-guilty feeling,
How your clarion voice goes pealing
Through the night.

Will H. Baigrie

Sustainers and Factors

COOKS

We may live without poetry, music and art;

We may live without conscience, and live without
heart;

We may live without friends; we may live without
books;

But civilized man cannot live without cooks.

We may live without books—what is knowledge but
grieving?

We may live without hope—what is hope but
deceiving?

We may live without love—what is passion but
pining?

But where is the man that can live without dining?

—*Owen Meredith*

From Lucile

God sends meat, the devil sends cooks.
—*Charles VI.*

A good cook has great power to assuage grief by his art.
—*Mouchy*

BREAD

Mankind have found the means to make grain into bread, the lightest and properest aliment for human bodies.
—*Arbuthnot*

WATER

Water is nature's carrier.
—*Maury*

Water is the fittest drink for all persons, of all ages and temperaments; of all the productions of nature or art, it comes the nearest to that universal remedy so much searched after by mankind but never discovered.
—*Charles Fenno Hoffman*

Water, soft pure graceful water! there is no shape into which you can throw her that she does not seem lovelier than before. Earth has no jewels so brilliant as her own spray; fire has no rubies like what she steals from the sunset; air has no robes like the grace of her ever-changing drapery of silver.
—*N. P. Willis*

[157]

SALT

O Salt! good to put into almost anything to eat or
drink.   What a piquancy you impart to a melon;
how savory is meat when touched by your magic;
how you coerce the best in milk and potatoes; how
you awaken the merry meditative oyster; how corn
and cucumbers and onions and fruits and tomatoes
are sent to the palate addressed with their true
flavor.   O Salt!

—Pseud.

Sports and Pastimes

SPORT

Life without sport is not life.

Mary Breese

Sport is a preserver of health.

—Crates

Sports are as necessary to divert the mind as the body.

—Philaiete

After serious matters let us indulge in a season of sport.

—Horace

Sports are a most excellent device with which to test a man's character.

—Olaus Magnus

PASTIMES

Gay day, play days, always hey days.
Childhood's a bubble.   Manhood is trouble.
Give us back play days, gay days, hey days,
Youth's laughing chime, romping and rhyme.
Ah, give them back to us, old Father Time.
—*Robert Emmet Mac Alarney,*
in "The Little Jade Joss"

Make a serious study of pastime.
—*Alexander the Great*

Pastime to a wise man is wisdom relaxing her
brow.
—*Arlotto*

PLAY

Be brisk at play.
—*Lyman Cobb*

It is better to play than do nothing.
—*Confucius*

Play, women and wine undo men laughing.
—*Chartier*

ANGLER'S REVEILLÉ

Sing trollillee, sing trollillee,
Where the trout streams flow,
And the breezes blow,
A-fishing, a-fishing, a-fishing we go.
—*Henry Warner*

ANGLING

Angling is an innocent cruelty.
—*George Parker*

God never did make a more calm, quiet, innocent recreation than angling.

—Izaak Walton

HUNTING

When we mount and away at the break of day,
　And we hie to the woodland side,
How the crash resounds as we cheer our hounds,
　And still at their sterns we ride.
　*　　*　　*　　*　　*　　*　　*
Then those that will may the bumper fill,
Or trace out the dance with glee;
But the steed's brave bound, and the opening hound,
And the rattling burst for me.

—Whyte Melville

Here's a health to all hunters, and long be their lives,
May they never be crost by their sweethearts or wives,
May they rule their own passions and ever at rest,
As the most happy men, be they also the best.
And free from all care which the many surrounds,
Be happy at last when they see no more hounds.

—Drexel Collection, in Lenox Library

HERE'S A HEALTH

Here's a health to them that can ride;
Here's a health to them that can ride!
And those who don't wish good luck to the cause
May they roast by their own fireside!

—Anon.

For now, when toils of chase are o'er,
   With many a near escape,
To Bacchus, jovial god, they pour
   The nectar of the grape.

               —Anon.
From The Sportsman's Vocal Cabinet
London, 1830

So push the bottle round, my boys,
   Ne'er let the wine stand still;
A fox-hunter his glass enjoys;
   Come, brother sportsmen, fill—
      And a-drinking we will go,
Now, farmers, doctors, majors, squires,
   And all good fellows here,
A bumper first my toast requires,
   Another standby to cheer—
     "To the Master of the Hounds."

               —Anon.

The bugle rings,
The sharp spur stings,
And the five-bar fence is done.
A swinging lope
Up the grassy slope,
The chase is just begun;
Oh, merry the galloping hoof tattoo,
The beat of the air in the face,
A steady eye and a stiffened wrist
As you ride for the fox and place.

       —Robert Emmet Mac Alarney

SAILING

And it's O for the sea and the sky!
  And it's O for the boat and the bay!
For the white foam whirling by,
  And the sharp, salt edge of the spray!
          —Austin Dobson

O'er the tranquil sea with fluttering sails, un-
harmed, rich fleets careen.
          —Horace

This quiet sail is as a noiseless wing
To waft me from distraction.
          —Byron

SWIMMING

O, a long, long stroke, with a stiff forearm,
And we shoulder the waves as we go.
With the salt on your lip, and the spray on your
    brow,
And a stroke that is steady and slow.
          —Robert Emmet Mac Alarney

HOOKEY

Here's to hookey and the son-of-a-gun
Who's played the game and knows it's fun.
Who's sat on the bank and fished all day,
Nor thought of the school-house far away.
          —Stanlicus

ROWING

Mr. Scholes is somewhere in Canada.

GOLF

Respectfully referred to W. J. Travis, care of—?

FOOTBALL

Waiting for the returns for the Fall of 1905.

BASEBALL

Here's to breezy baseball!
The finest game of all.

*   *   *   *   *

Look at the lay of the glorious green,
Marked here and there with men in between,—
Eager, expectant,—"Oh! my, what a run!"
Chasing the spheroid across the sun.
     "Hurrah! hi, hi!"
     "Observe that fly!"
     ("Two to one.")

—Pseud.

EXERCISE

Keep the body in health by exercise.

—Cleobulus

A man must exercise or fast, or take physic or be sick.

—Sir William Temple

Exercise is the chief source of improvement in our faculties.

—Hugh Blair

POLO

Here's to Polo! a game for Centaurs.

—Stanlicus

CHESS

Chess is a wooden or ivory allegory.

—Chatfield

In the game of chess we illustrate the game of life and its vicissitudes—success and failure.

—Opoix

TERPSICHORE

In narrowest girdle, O reluctant Muse,
In closest frock and Cinderella shoes,
Bound to the foot-lights for thy brief display,
One zephyr step and then dissolve away!

—Oliver Wendell Holmes

Blest relaxation of the nerves,
Improver of the eye!
Long at your shrine the tyro serves,
Loud sounds his gusty sigh.
In deep distress he bangs and swears
And drives with savage power.
Relentlessly a big clock stares,
Displayed above, a grim sign bears:
" Sixty cents an hour."

—Henry Stanley Haskins

Libations and Potations

With beaded bubbles winking at the brim,
And purple-stained mouth.

—Keats

WINE

Come, come, good wine is a good familiar creature, if it be well used.

—Shakespeare

Let us have wine and women, mirth and laughter,
Sermons and soda-water the day after.

—Byron

Good wine needs no bush.

—Shakespeare

Wine that maketh glad the heart of man.

—Old Testament

Across the walnuts and the wine.

—Tennyson

DRINK TO ME ONLY WITH THINE EYES

Libations and Potations

Andantino

Drink to me only with thine eyes, And
I will pledge with mine; Or leave a kiss within the cup, And I'll not ask for wine. The
thirst that from the soul doth rise, Doth
ask a drink di - vine; But might I of Jove's
nectar sup, I would not change for thine.

I sent thee late a rosy wreath,
    Not so much honouring thee,
As giving it a hope that there
    It could not withered be ;

But thou thereon didst only breathe,
    And sent'st it back to me ;
Since when it grows, and smells, I swear,
    Not of itself, but thee.—*Ben Jonson*

[167]

WINE

Go fetch to me a pint o' wine,
  And fill it in a silver tassie,
That I may drink before I go,
  A service to the bonnie lassie.

—Burns

When the early mass is all passed and said
And we leave the church with its silent dead,
We think of the capons roasting slow,
On the turning spit with the flames aglow;
Of the casks of wine in the cellar dim
With its smooth worn floor and its arches grim.
—Robert Emmet Mac Alarney,
from "Ye Mayde of Yorke"

Here's to wine—safer outside than in.
—Stanlicus

It has become quite a common proverb that
in wine there is truth.

—Pliny the Elder

Fill the bowl with rosy wine,
Around our temples roses twine,
And let us cheerfully awhile,
Like the wine and roses, smile.
To-day is ours; what do we fear?
To-day is ours; we have it here!
Let's banish business, banish sorrow,
To the gods belongs to-morrow.

—Cowley

[168]

Send hither wine and rich perfume,
And the loved rose's short-lived bloom,
While wealth is thine, and youthful years.
—*Horace.*

Drinking with purpled lip the nectar of the gods.
—*Horace*

Enter, 'mong peaceful gods to find a home
And quaff 'mid star-bright skies the nectar juice
divine.
—*Horace*

Why not at ease beneath this pine
Our whitening hair with roses twine,
And quaff the rich Falernian wine?
—*Horace*

Give me champagne! and contentment be mine!
  Women, wealth, and ambition—I cast them away.
My garlanded forehead let vine-trees entwine!
  And life shall to me be one long summer's day.
With the tears of the clustering grape for its rain,
And in sunshine—the bright golden floods of cham-
    pagne!
—*Whyte Melville*

To the expecting mouth, with grateful taste,
The ebbing wine glides swiftly o'er the tongue.
—*John Gay*

Haste;
A cask unbroached of mellow wine
Awaits thee, roses interlaced,
And perfumes pressed from nard divine.

—Horace

What dreaming drone was ever blest
  By thinking of the morrow?
To-day be mine—I leave the rest
  To all the fools of sorrow;
Then, brother soldier, fill the wine,
  Fill high the wine to beauty;
Love, friendship, honour, all are thine,
  Thy country and thy duty.

—W. Smyth

Had Neptune, when first he took charge of the sea,
Been as wise or at least been as merry as we,
He'd have thought better on't and instead of his
  brine
Would have filled up the vast ocean with generous
  wine.

—Anon.

Bacchus drowns within the bowl
Troubles that corrode the soul.

—Horace

Here in the golden sparkling wine,
I toast my loved one's lips,
Which make the wine, howe'er divine,
Fade in eclipse.
                    —*Philip McAllister*

No wine for me!—Nay, an' it be thy will,
Kiss first the goblet—I will drink my fill:
How may I, when thy lips have touched it, dare
Be sober still.
                    —*William M. Hardinge*

Fill me my wine in crystal; thus, and thus
I see't in's *puris naturalibus:*
Unmix'd.   I love to have it smirk and shine;
'Tis sin I know, 'tis sin to throttle wine.
                    —*Robert Herrick*

    Oft have we
Beguiled the lingering day, each brow
Glistening with nard of Araby,
And quaffed the wine.
                    —*Horace*

TO BURGUNDY

Hail, Burgundy, thou juice divine,
    Inspirer of my song:—
The praises given to other wine
    To thee alone belong.
Of poignant wit and rosy charms,
    Thou can'st the power improve,
Care of its sting thy balm disarms,
    Thou noblest gift of Jove!
—*Inscribed to the Musical Society, at the
        Five Bells Tavern in the Strand*

[171]

**Libations
and
Potations**

Slaves! the beaker fill once more
　With potent draughts of Massic wine!
Forth from shells capacious pour
　Indian essences divine.

—Horace

Close we stand as we drink and pledge in the glowing
　wine—
No warm Naiad, I think, need kiss in your cup or
　mine.

—William M. Hardinge

Heap high the logs!　Pour forth with lavish hand,
　O Thaliarchus, draughts of long-stored wine,
　Blood of the Sabine vine!
To-day be ours; the rest the gods command.

—Horace

TO BACCHUS

Come, jolly god Bacchus, here's to thee,
　Huzza! boys, huzza! boys, huzza!
Sing Io, sing Io, to Bacchus.
　Hence, all ye dull thinkers, withdraw.
Come, what should we do but be jovial,
　Come, tune up your voices and sing.
What soul is so dull to be heavy
　When wine sets our fancies on wing.

—From the Merry Bacchanalian
(An old English song)

A BACCHANALIAN TOAST

Drink up
Your cup,
But not spill wine;
For if you
        Do
'Tis an ill sign.

—Robert Herrick

HUNTING THE BOTTLE

Then charge your glasses merrily round,
Since we're supplied with hare and hound,
While cheerful Bacchus leads us on,
We'll follow in chorus with sprightly
Ton, ton, ton, ton.

—Anon.

TO QUAFF AND REST

A simple myrtle-fillet twine
    For me, for both; it suits us best,
As, shadowed by the matted vine
    I quaff the ruby wine, and rest.

—Horace

SAE BEWITCHING

There's death in the cup—sae beware!
    Nay, more—there is danger in touching;
But wha can avoid the fell snare?
    The man and his wine's sae bewitching.

—Robert Burns

[173]

FILL THE BUMPER FAIR

Fill the bumper fair!
  Every drop we sprinkle
O'er the brow of Care
  Smoothes away a wrinkle.
Wit's electric flame
  Ne'er so swiftly passes,
As when through the frame
  It shoots from brimming glasses.

Fill the bumper fair!
  Every drop we sprinkle
O'er the brow of Care
  Smoothes away a wrinkle.

—*Moore*

HAIL! GENIAL KING!

Bacchus! To thee belong
The glories twain of peace and war,
The fight, the jest, the dance, the song;
  Hail! Genial king!

—*Horace*

BACCHUS

O Bacchus! let us be
From cares and troubles free;
And thou shalt hear how we
Will chant new hymns to thee.

—*Robert Herrick*

[174]

FIVE WINES

Brisk methinks I am, and fine
When I drink my cap'ring wine;
Then to love I do incline,
When I drink my wanton wine;
And I wish all maidens mine,
When I drink my sprightly wine;
Well I sup and well I dine,
When I drink my frolic wine;
But I languish, lower, and pine,
When I want my fragrant wine.
—*Robert Herrick*

AULON'S VINE

Where friendly Aulon's vine
To Bacchus from her purple bosom yields
Nectar more rich than best Falernian wine.
—*Horace*

A TOAST, B. C. 30

Drink, comrades, drink; give loose to mirth!
With joyous footstep beat the earth,
And spread before the War-God's shrine
The Salian feast, the sacrificial wine.
—*Horace*

GARRYOWEN

Let Bacchus's sons be not dismayed,
But join with me each jovial blade;
Come booze and sing, and lend your aid
To help me with the chorus.
—*Anon.*

[175]

WREATHE THE BOWL

Wreathe the bowl
With flowers of soul,
The brightest Wit can find us;
   We'll take a flight
   Towards heav'n to-night,
And leave dull earth behind us.

—Moore

PATHS UNTROD

Whither through wastes unscanned by mortal eye
Bear'st thou me, Bacchus; through what paths
   untrod?

—Horace

SONG OF THE VINE

This song of mine is a song of the vine,
   To be sung by glowing embers
Of wayside inns, when the rain begins
   To darken the drear Novembers.

—Longfellow

GROG

For grog is our larboard and starboard,
Our mainmast, our mizzen, our log,
At sea, or ashore, or when harbored,
The mariners' compass is grog.

—Anon.

BEER

And here's a pot of good double beer, neighbour,
Drink and fear not your man.

—Henry VI. (Part II)

[176]

RUM

He who drinks one glass a day,
Will live to die some other way.

Stanlicus

ALE-CASK

Oh, many a man has drunk to his bride,
And a bonnie fair maid she may be.
But I give a health to the ale that I quaff,
For my ale-cask is married to me,
Ha! ha! for my ale-cask is married to me.

If the wind in the night, in the wild stormy night,
Salt with spray, sings a sailor's farewell,
I pile on the logs, and I fill up my glass
And I troll like a monk in his cell,
Ha! ha! and I troll like a monk in his cell.

—Henry Stanley Haskins

THE GOBLET

Fill high the goblet! Envious Time
Steals, as we speak, our fleeting prime.
Away with hope! Away with sorrow!
Snatch thou to-day, nor trust to-morrow.

—Horace

WHISKEY

Whiskey, drink divine!
Why should drivellers bore us
With the praise of wine,
Whilst we've thee before?

—Joseph O'Leary

[177]

TO TOM AND JERRY

In Spring I sing the fine May wine;
In summer, mint and sherry;
Good rye, when Autumn's breezes blow;
But, chilled by winter's sleet and snow,
I call for Tom and Jerry.

—Winifred Fales

THE TINKER'S TOAST

Along, come along,
Let's meet in a throng
    Here of tinkers;
And quaff up a bowl
As big as a cowl
    To beer drinkers.

—Robert Herrick

COBBLER'S TOAST

Come sit we by the fire's side,
    And roundly drink we here;
Till that we see our cheeks ale-dyed
    And noses tann'd with beer.

—Robert Herrick

CUP O' KINDNESS

And surely ye'll be your pint-stoup,
    And surely I'll be mine;
And we'll tak a cup o' kindness yet,
    For auld lang syne.

—Robert Burns

[178]

SATURDAY NIGHT AT SEA

Come, messmates, fill the cheerful bowl!
  To-night let no one fail,
No matter how the billows roll,
  Or roars the ocean gale.
There's toil and danger in our lives,
  But let us jovial be,
And drink to sweethearts and to wives
  On Saturday night at sea!

—Bayard Taylor

DRINKING SONG

Fill, lads, fill;
Fill, lads, fill.
Here we have a cure
  For every ill.
If Fortune's unkind
As the north-east wind,
Still we must endure,
Trusting to our cure,
  In better luck still.

—Frederick Marryat

TRUE BLUE

I hope there's no soul
Met over this bowl
But means honest ends to pursue:
  With the voice and the heart
  Let us never depart
From the faith of an honest true blue, true blue.

—Jacobite Toast

FIVE REASONS

If on my theme I rightly think,
There are five reasons why men drink,—
Good wine, a friend, because I'm dry,
Or lest I should be by and by,
Or any other reason why.

—John Sirmond, 1589-1649

NE'ER THINK ON TO-MORROW

Good liquor will banish all niggardly care—
And a song that is jovial the spirits will cheer.
O'er a song and a bumper then let us be gay.
Ne'er think of to-morrow, but drink, boys, to-day.

—Anon.

THE TOPER

When I drink the spacious bowl,
Drinking, I enlarge my soul;
And with young men ever gay,
Dance and am as young as they.

—From an old song

AN CRUISCIN LAN*

Let the farmer praise his grounds,
Let the huntsman praise his hounds,
    The shepherd his dew-scented lawn;
But I, more blest than they,
Spend each happy night and day
    With my charming little *cruiscin lan, lan, lan,*
    My charming little *cruiscin lan.*

—Anon.

An cruiskeen lawn.   The little full jug.

[180]

JOHN BARLEYCORN

Then let us toast John Barleycorn,
  Each man a glass in hand;
And may his great posterity
  Ne'er fail in old Scotland!
                    —*Robert Burns*

'TIS TO THEE

Were't the last drop in the well,
  As I gasped upon the brink,
Ere my fainting spirit fell,
  'Tis to thee that I would drink.
                    —*Byron*

TO RIVAL MONKS

I cannot eat but little meat,
  My stomach is not good;
But sure I think that I can drink
  With him that wears a hood.
—*John Still: "Gammer Gurton's Needle"*

FILL THE RED BOWL

      Care, like a dun,
      Lurks at the gate:
      Let the dog wait;
      Happy we'll be!
      Drink every one;
      Pile up the coals,
      Fill the red bowls,
      Round the old tree!
                    —*Thackeray*

DRAIN OUR BARRELS DRY

Fill, fill your glasses high,
We'll drain our barrels dry;
Out upon them, fie! fie!
That winna do't again.

—Jaeobite Toast

TAVERN

Taverns are places where madness is sold by the bottle.

—Swift

A tavern is a house kept for those who are not housekeepers.

—Chatfield

A tavern is an inn, the free rendezvous of all travellers, and where the humor of each displays itself, without ceremony or restraint.

—Scott

THE TAVERN SIGN

I have heard that on a day
Mine host's signboard flew away,

* * * * * * *

I sat
Underneath a new old-sign
Sipping beverage divine,
And pledging with contented smack
The Mermaid in the Zodiac.

—Keats

Sonnets

By FRANCIS SALTUS SALTUS

Water

I hear strange voices in the warm, swift rain,
  That falls in tumult upon town and field;
  It seems to tell a mystery unconcealed,
Yet hieroglyphic to a mortal's brain.

It sighs and moans as if in utter pain
  Of some colossal sorrow, never healed;
  It warns of awful secrets unrevealed,
And every drop repeats the sad refrain.

And then I think of the enormous sea
  Fed by these drops, with drifting wrecks bestrewn,
And dimly, vaguely, like a far-off sound,
The meaning of their sorrow comes to me,
  For they may be, Oh rare, considerate boon,
Heaven's humble mourners for the unnumbered
    drowned.

—Francis Saltus Saltus

Beer

What merry fairy, oh cool, delicious beer,
Gave thee the power through centuries to maintain
A charm that soothes dull care, and laughs at pain;
A power sad hearts to vitalize and cheer?
No blasé palate of thy drops can fear;
Once quaffed, lips eager, seek thy sweets again,
Without thee students sing no loud refrain;
Laughter and mirth depart, be thou not near.
And when I drink thee to my soul's delight,
A vision of King Gambrinus, fat and gay,
Haunts me, and I behold bright tankards shine,
And hear him laugh with many a thirsty wight,
And merry maidens, drinking night and day,
In quaint old gabled towns along the Rhine.

—Francis Saltus Saltus

Ale

Whene'er thy foaming beads attract my lips,
A rapid vision passes o'er my mind
Of strong Cunarders, battling with the wind,
And cozy cabins, and the roll of ships.
I hear the tempest lash the sails like whips,
I see the rigid bow its pathway find
Deep in the night, leaving in sheen behind
A snaky trail of phosphorescent tips.
Or, when thy vigor to the lees I drain,
I, from the belfry of St. Paul's behold
Gigantic London in gray winter hours,
Waiting for drowsy dawn to come again,
While the great sun, veiled in a fog of gold,
Bursts in red glory on her haughty Towers!

—Francis Saltus Saltus

Port

When unto me they bring, with gentle care,
Thy nectar, sleeping in the cobwebbed flask,
There is no boon of fairy gods to ask
More pain annihilating or more rare.
The gloomy gray of storm-clouds seemeth fair,
Thou makest light the long day's onerous task.
Uplifted lies life's tedium and its mask,
Light, love and laughter enter everywhere.
And then I see old bankers, flushed with pride,
Converse on politics, and gold and Pitt;
But cheerier far, in some dim tavern's nook,
I see in dreams dear Jerrold, by the side
Of glorious Thackeray, listening to the wit,
And gay, infectious laugh of Theodore Hook.

—Francis Saltus Saltus

Coffee

Voluptuous berry! Where may mortals find
Nectars divine that can with thee compare,
When, having dined, we sip thy essence rare,
And feel toward wit and repartee inclined?

Thou wert of sneering, cynical Voltaire
The only friend; thy power urged Balzac's mind
To glorious effort; surely Heaven designed
Thy devotees superior joys to share.

Whene'er I breathe thy fumes, 'mid Summer stars,
The Orient's splendent pomps my vision greet.
Damascus with its myriad minarets gleams!
I see thee, smoking in immense bazars,
Or yet in dim seraglios, at the feet
Of blond Sultanas, pale with amorous dreams !

—Francis Saltus Saltus

Tea

From what enchanted Eden came thy leaves
That hide such subtle spirits of perfume?
Did eyes pre-adamite first see thee bloom,
Luscious nepenthe of the soul that grieves?

By thee the tired and torpid mind conceives,
Fairer than roses brightening life's gloom,
Thy protean charm can every form assume
And turn December nights to April eves.

Thy amber-tinted drops bring back to me
Fantastic shapes of great Mongolian towers,
Emblazoned banners, and the booming gong;
I hear the sound of feast and revelry,
And smell, far sweeter than the sweetest flowers,
The Kiosks of Pekin, fragrant of Oolong!

—Francis Saltus Saltus

Champagne

Delicious, effervescent, cold Champagne,
Imprisoned sunshine, glorious and bright,
How many virtues in thy charm unite?
Who from thy tempting witchery can abstain?

Sad hearts by *ennui* vexed revive again
When in the frail, green glass thou foamest light,
And by the spell our sophistry takes flight;
Fair queen of wines, long be thy merry reign!

To me thy sparkling souvenir recalls
Grand Boulevards, all dazzling with the glare
Of countless lights; the revel and uproar
Of midnight Paris and the opera balls;
A maze of masks! A challenge flung to Care!
And charming suppers at the ''Maison d'Or.''

—*Francis Saltus Saltus*

Irish Whiskey

From Cork to Tipperary and Tralee,
There's been more laughter, jollity and fun
Than yet's been known beneath the risen sun
In all the world together, born of thee!

Thou bring'st out finely the old Celtic glee,
Yarns, jokes and glorious bulls surpassed by
    none,
Side-splitting stories, funny when begun,
And at the end one royal mental spree.

And when I drink thee quite alone, ('tis rare),
I picture up a host of merry men,
Tasting thy charm and joking without stint,
And recognize the Hoods and Jerrolds there
Who, gay and careless, never take a pen,
But cast their gems beyond the grasp of print!

                —Francis Saltus Saltus

Scotch Whiskey

How rare is thy rich, passion-giving worth,
When weary of full many a Scottish mile,
One rests, and stirs thee with a knowing smile
In some dim inn of Edinburgh or Perth.

Gods must have drunk thee at their wondrous birth,
For in thee there is laughter and no guile,
And they, enraptured, from some heavenly aisle,
Perchance have given thee to this sorrowing earth.

For when thou art near, the devil has the pain,
No bitter frown is known, no caustic sneer,
The world on golden axles moves and turns.
And then ring out again, and yet again,
In manly accents, resolute and clear,
The immortal songs and glees of Bobby Burns!

—*Francis Saltus Saltus*

Brandy

Thy mighty power stirs up the sluggish blood
To craft and cunning and rejuvenate fire,
And fills again with raptures of desire
The failing sense that drowns in amour's flood.

Thy spirit's song, freed from our carnal mud,
Then soars supreme, and grandlier doth aspire,
And with new vigor that can never tire,
The flower of fancy burst within the bud.

In nobler ways, even yet, thou prov'st thy might,
When soldiers, strengthened by thy drops of flame
Forget their gory wounds in frantic zeal,
And with high souls all thrilling for the fight,
Assault dread bastions for their country's fame,
And lead their flags thro' labyrinths of steel !

> —*Francis Saltus Saltus*

Chocolate

Liquid delectable, I love thy brown
Deep-glimmering color like a wood-nymph's tress;
Potent and swift to urge on Love's excess,
Thou wert most loved in the fair Aztec town

Where Cortes, battling for Iberia's crown,
First found thee, and with rough and soldier guess,
Pronounced thy virtues of rare worthiness
And fit by Madrid's dames to gain renown.

When tasting of thy sweets, fond memories
Of bygone days in Versailles will arise;
Before the King, reclining at his ease,
I see Dubarry in rich toilet stand,
A gleam of passion in her lustrous eyes,
A Sevres cup held in her jeweled hand!

—Francis Saltus Saltus

Tokai

A glass of thy reviving gold to me,
Whether or no my dreamy soul be sad,
Brings souvenirs of lovely Vienna, glad
In her eternal summer-time to be!

I hear, in joyous trill, resounding free,
The waltzes that the German fairies bade
The souls of Strauss and Lanier, music mad,
Compose, to set the brains of worlds aglee.

And in the Sperl, dreaming away the sweet
Of pleasant life, and finding it all praise,
Dead to the past and scorning Death's surprise,
I see in calm felicity complete
Some fair Hungarian Jewess on me gaze
With the black glory of Hebraic eyes!

                    —*Francis Saltus Saltus*

Nicotiana

Here's to you and your cigar; light it well and the Recording Angel will have less to do.
> —*M. E. Flaherty*

Tobacco helps the memory.
> —*Magliabecchi*

Take no physic but tobacco, which is a cure for almost all distempers.
> —*De Foe*

What a glorious creature was he who first discovered the use of tobacco!
> —*Fielding*

There is a certain relish in the smoking of tobacco, which only smokers know.
> —*Robertson*

The daintiest dish of a delicious feast,
By taking which man differs from a beast.
> —*Anon.: Time, James I.*

Nicotiana

Happy mortal! He who knows
Pleasure which a pipe bestows;
Curling eddies climb the room,
Wafting round a mild perfume.
—Isaac Hawkins Browne

This makes me sing, soho, soho, boyes,
  Ho, boyes, sound I loudly;
Earth ne'er did breed
Such a jovial weed,
  Whereof to boast so proudly!
—Barton Holiday

The mighty Thebe and Babylon the great,
Imperial Rome, in turn, have bowed to fate;
So this great world and each particular star
Must all burn out, like you, my last cigar:
A puff—a transient fire, that ends in smoke.
And all that's given to man—that bitter joke—
Youth, Hope and Love, three whiffs of passing zest,
Then come the ashes, and the long, long rest.
—Henry James Meller

Hail! social pipe—thou foe to care,
Companion of my elbow chair;
As forth thy curling fumes arise,
They seem an evening sacrifice—
An offering to my Maker's praise,
For all his benefits and grace.
—Dr. Garth: A Long Time Ago

[198]

I like cigars
Beneath the stars,
Upon the waters blue.
To sing and float,
While rocks the boat—
Upon the waves—don't you?

To rest the oar,
And float to shore—
While soft the moonbeams shine—
To laugh and joke
And idly smoke,
I think is quite divine.

> —*Ella Wheeler Wilcox*
> *Written in a friend's album*

INSCRIPTIONS FOR TOBACCO JARS

Do you recall the wondrous brazen vase
Fish'd up long since in an Arabian Night,
Whence rose a thick columnar smoke, that was
A fearful Djinn of more than mortal might?
I am akin to it—within my womb,
Hid in the fragrant stores therein that be,
There dwells a kindly genius, that from fume,
Becomes to man embodied!

> —*Anon.: Reverie*

Keep me at hand and as my fumes arise,
You'll find a *jar* the gates of paradise.

> —*Anon.*

SUBLIME SMOKING

Sublime tobacco! which from east to west
Cheers the tar's labour or the Turkman's rest;
Which on the Moslem's ottoman divides
His hours, and rivals opiums and his brides;
Magnificent in Stamboul, but less grand,
Though not less loved, in Wapping or the Strand;
Divine in hookahs, glorious in a pipe,
When tipped with amber, mellow, rich, and ripe;
Like other charmers, wooing the caress
More dazzlingly when daring in full dress;
Yet thy true lovers more admire by far
Thy naked beauties—Give me a cigar!
                    —Byron: The Island, Canto II.

A PIPE OF TOBACCO

Let the learned talk of books,
The glutton of cooks,
    The lover of Celia's soft smack—O!
No mortal can boast
So noble a toast
    As a pipe of accepted tobacco!
                    —Henry Fielding

THE BEST PIPE

Clay, meerschaum, hookah, what are they
    That I should view them with desire?
I'll sing, till all my hair is gray,
    Give me a finely seasoned briar.
                    —R. F. Murray

[200]

THE PIPE TO THE SNUFF-BOX

My breath is as sweet as the breath of blown roses,
  While you are a nuisance where'er you appear;
There is nothing but snivelling and blowing of noses,
  Such a noise as turns any man's stomach to hear.
                              —*William Cowper*

Let him who has a mistress to her eyebrow write a
      sonnet,
Let the lover of a lily pen a languid ode upon it;
In such sentimental subjects I'm a Philistine and
      cynic,
And prefer the inspiration drawn from sources nico-
      tinic.
                              —*Arthur W. Grundy*

AFTER-DINNER CLOUD

What wonder if I envy not
  The rich, the giddy, and the proud,
Contented in this quiet spot
  To blow my after-dinner cloud?
                          —*Henry S. Leigh*

RALEIGH'S HERB

Blessings on old Raleigh's head—
  Though upon the block it fell—
For the knowledge he first spread
  Of the herb I love so well!
                          —*Anon.*

SCORN NOT THE MEERSCHAUM

Scorn not the meerschaum.   Housewives, you have
    croaked
In ignorance of its charms.   Through this small reed
Did Milton now and then consume the weed;
The poet Tennyson hath oft evoked
The Muse with glowing pipe, and Thackeray joked
And wrote and sang in nicotinian mood;
Hawthorne with this hath cheered his solitude;
A thousand times this pipe hath Lowell smoked;
Full oft hath Aldrich, Stoddard, Taylor, Cranch
And many more whose verses float about,
Puffed the Virginian or Havana leaf;
And when the poet's or the artist's branch
Drops no sustaining fruit, how sweet to pout
Consolatory whiffs—alas too brief!

                            —Anon.

ON A BROKEN PIPE

Neglected now it lies, a cold clay form,
So late with living inspirations warm;
Type of all other creatures formed of clay—
What more than it for Epitaph have they?
                        —James Thomson

GERMAN SMOKING SONG.

When love grows cool, thy fire still warms me;
When friends are fled, thy presence charms me.
If thou art full, though purse be bare,
I smoke and cast away all care!

                            —Anon.

CLOUDS

Mortals say their hearts are light
When the clouds around disperse;
Clouds to gather thick as night,
Is the smoker's universe.
                    —*From the German of Bauerfield*

OLD PIPE OF MINE

Let others seek the bliss that reigns
    In homage paid at beauty's shrine,
We envy not such foolish gains,
    In sweet content, old pipe of mine.
                    —*John J. Gormley*

Consolers, Healers and Counsellors

MINISTERS

A good minister and a good father may well agree together.

—T. Fuller

The Christian ministry is the worst of all trades, but the best of all professions.

—J. Newton

A minister is God's ambassador.

—Miles Smith

PRIESTS

The people who have no priests are commonly barbarians.

—Montesquieu

The priesthood is a celestial honor, not an earthly but a heavenly procession

—Philo

DOCTORS

A doctor—good doctor—is the aide-de-camp of life.

—*Anon.*

Unto our doctors let us drink,
Who cure our chills and ills,
No matter what we really think
About their bills and pills.
—*Philip McAllister*

LAWYERS

Without lawyers it would be necessary that every person engaged in a lawsuit should be his own advocate, which would expose him to many evils.
—*Theodore Dwight*

Why, gentlemen, you cannot live without the lawyers, and certainly you cannot die without them.
—*Joseph H. Choate*
(*Quotation from a speech on "The Bench and Bar"*)

Customs, Comforts and Luxuries

CUSTOMS

Old Customs! Oh! I love the sound
However simple they may be:
Whate'er with time hath sanction found,
Is welcome and is dear to me.
Pride grows above simplicity,
And spurns them from her haughty mind,
And soon the poet's song will be
The only refuge they can find.

—Clare

I drink it as the Fates ordain it,
Come, fill it, and have done with rhymes;
Fill up the lonely glass, and drain it
In memory of dear old times.

—Thackeray

Custom is the universal sovereign.

—Pindarus

Custom is a most powerful master.

—Pliny

Custom has an ascendency over the understanding.

—Isaac Watts

HOME

There is no place like home.

—John Howard Payne

A well-regulated home is a millennium on a small scale.

—Talmage

There is something in that little word "home," which lifts the heart into the throat, and ever excites intense emotion.

—Robert Bickersteth

EATING

In good eating there is happiness.

—Apicus

A man must eat though every tree were a gallows.
—C. M. Clarke

He who eats with most pleasure is he who least requires sauce.

—Xenophon

The chief pleasure in eating does not consist in costly seasoning or exquisite flavor but in yourself.
—Horace

[207]

BREAKFAST

A little in the morning is enough.

—The Cid

DINNER

Dinners ought to be by all means encouraged among officials of government, for the well-being of a state rests upon the foundation of reciprocal hospitality.

—R. B. Todd

A good dinner sharpens wit, while it softens the heart.

—John Doran

AFTER DINNER

When the cloth is cleared and a suave Havana points its spiral finger heavenwards, our thoughts, like gymnasts, scale the rings of smoke; then, as drowsy children, make ready for bed.

—Stanlicus

SUPPER

A supper is a receipt for indigestion and a sleepless night.

Light suppers make long life.

—Damhouder

SATURDAY NIGHT

How pleasant is Saturday night when you've tried all the week to be good.

—Anon.

CHAFING-DISH

We'll drink to the rabbit.   The rabbit—no jack.
And tinted a soft melting yellow divine,
With lingering breath that bespeaks Paradise,
'Tis a cup far more cheering than pledges in wine.

—*Robert Emmet Mac Alarney*

TO MY OLD HAT

And thou hast clasped my marble brow,
   And daily sunk still deeper down
Until thy brim doth hide me now
   From lofty sneer and worldly frown!
Thou once wert black—who now art brown,
   But what care I for aught of that?
Thou art thy owner's rightful crown,
   My trusty friend—my ancient hat!

And I must buy another tile,
   To catch the scoffer's quizzing glance,
With modern crown of pattern vile,
   Distorted brim—just born of France!
It will not fit me well, perchance;
   E'en you were years before you sat
In ease my beauty to enhance,
   My trusty friend—my ancient hat!

L'ENVOI

Ah me!   Too much this haunting fear
   Before I give thee to the cat
I'll wear thee for another year,
   My trusty friend—my ancient hat!

—*Anon.*

THE BATH

The bath is a great medicine.

—*Dr. Daniel Wilson*

There is scarcely a religious system into which bathing has not been introduced.

—*Dr. William Alexander*

Here's to you—Turkish Bath,
  How restful you are—"altogether."
You certainly cut a wide swath,
  When you turn on your samples of weather.

You know what is good for the blood,
  When you send in your flow of "hot stuff"—
But here's the man sending a flood—
  "Come, rubber! a plunge! I've enough."

—*Pseud.*

The morning bath is a great tonic, a luxury, a necessity, a cleanser, a satisfaction, a gratification —besides it's lots of fun!

—*Pseud.*

THE EASY CHAIR

O, easy chair, O, easy chair!
  What rhymes with my old friend?
I only know that toil and care,
  In thee both have their end—
For in thy yielding arms and back,
  I feel thy gentle might,
And far from all the grind and rack,
  I doze, and say "good night!"

—*Pseud.*

DRESS

Dress does not give knowledge.

—*Truate*

Dress has a moral effect on the conduct of mankind.

—*Sir John Barrington*

As a rough shell covers a pearl, so does a man's dress cover the upright and noble.

—*Al Rashid*

Dress yourself fine where others are fine and plain where others are plain, but take care—that your clothes fit you.

—*Chesterfield*

CONVERSATION

Conversation is a ventilation of the heart.

—*Irico*

Conversation teaches more than meditation.

—*Schiller*

Repose is as necessary in conversation as in a picture.

—*Hazlitt*

Conversation is a relaxation, and not a fencing school or a game of chess.

—*D'Alembert*

[211]

COMMON-SENSE

Common-sense is of itself an income.
—*George Webbe*

Common-sense is a rare commodity.
—*Edward Moore*

Common-sense is Nature's gift, but reason is an art.
—*Beattie*

Common-sense is the best indication of a sound mind.
—*Dr. Cheyne*

Wherewithal

MONEY

Money rules the world.

—*Justin*

O money! money! how blindly thou hast been worshipped, and how stupidly abused! Thou art health and liberty and strength, and he that has thee may rattle defiance at the foul fiend.

—*Lamb*

Money is a king without a title.

—*Anna F. Canfield*

Money is a handmaiden if thou knowest how to use it; a mistress if thou knowest not.

—*Horace*

Fight thou with shafts of silver and o'ercome,
When no force else can get the masterdom.

—*Robert Herrick*

Fortune's a blind profuser of her own,
Too much she gives to some, enough to none.
—Robert Herrick

When all birds else do of their music fail,
Money's the still sweet-singing nightingale.
—Robert Herrick

GOLD

Gold is the picklock that never fails.
—Massinger

Gold has greater power over men than ten thousand arguments.
—Euripides

Gold gives to the ugliest a certain charm, and without it everything else is a miserable affair.
—Anon.

Gold can make its way through the midst of guards and break through the strongest barriers more easily than the lightning's bolt.
—Horace

Gold weighed 'gainst Honor is naught in the scale
—Ruckert

TRUE RICHES

True riches mean not revenue.
—Horace

ENOUGH

Happy is he whose modest means afford enough
—no more.
—Horace

POVERTY

Give Want her welcome if she comes; we find
Riches to be but burdens to the mind.
—Robert Herrick

ECONOMY

Economy is of itself a great revenue.
—Cicero

Economy is simply the art of getting the worth
of your money.
Anon.

Without economy none can be rich, and with it
few can be poor.
—Dr. Johnson

TO THE BOSTON PAPA

"I wish," he said, "you could make pies
Like mother used to bake."
"And I," said she, "wish that you made
The dough pa used to make!"
—Anon.

Utilities

THE CLOCK

Clocks sound the march of generations; a time to be born, as well as a time to die.

—*Talmage*

Gravest of moralists, loudest of preachers, most inflexible, the most equitable of despots, the clock resides in a lofty place; he reigns supreme over his own church and people; he is sole defender of the parish faith; he is a just, yet a paternal king.

—*Arethusa*

THE PEN

The pen is the tongue of the mind.

—*Cervantes*

The pen is both a rod and a sceptre.

—*Aretino*

The pen is a faithful companion to a great mind.
— *Mary Ann Hammer Dodd*

The pen is a formidable weapon, but a man can ill himself with it a great deal more easily than he an other people.
—*George Denison Prentice*

THE OLD COFFEE-POT

I want to hear the simmer
  Of the old coffee-pot;
I want to hear it hummin',
  When it's gettin' good and hot;
I want to see the vapor rise,
  Like incense in the room,
And float about a-fillin'
  Every corner with perfume.

I love the smell of roses
  Along about in June;
And I'd hang around and listen
  To almost any tune;
But the fragrance and the music
  That nothin' else has got
Are the odor and the simmer
  Of the old coffee-pot.
      —*John W. Fellows*

PHOTOGRAPHY

Photography and writing comfort the absent.
      —*Edward Parsons Day*

THE TELEPHONE

Here's to you!
Cheers to you,
Telephone!
Rancor
And
Spite
And a mighty
Sight
Of
Tender sighs
And
Business lies
Have come
And gone
Along your
Copper highway.
It's nobody's
Biz,
But
Gee Whiz! Think
Of the
Kisses of
1000's of
Misses
You've had.
Execrable
Taste to
Waste
A kiss on
You—thing of

Rubber and
Steel
And
Revolving
Wheel and
Diaphragm.
You're only a
Sham.
You haven't
Tongue
Or a
Lung,
And yet you
SPEAK!
You haven't
An ear, and
Yet you
HEAR!
Some day you
May
Get
Gay.
And say,
What you'll
Tell will—
Well—
Raise
HELL—O
Central,
Ring off!

—Henry Stanley Haskins, in "Life"

TELEGRAPH

The telegraph has conquered time.
                    —*S. F. B. Morse*

The telegraph is the triumph and marvel of our
day.
                    —*Henry Ward Beecher*

By means of the magnetic telegraph the people of
our country are holding a continuous mass-meeting.
                    —*Wendell Phillips*

ELECTRICITY

Electricity pervades all matter.
                    —*Maverick*

Electricity and steam have brought the ends of
the earth together, and the antipodes speak face to
face and exchange products.
                    —*Albert Leighton Rawson*

TO A THERMOMETER

O, thing of high and low degree,
We raise a tribute unto thee;
When heat clouds dot the summer sky,
You mount your narrow staircase high.
When winter winds their trumpets blow,
You turn your steps and go below.
Grim arbiter of human ills,
Of swimming brows and icy chills!
                    —*Henry Stanley Haskins*

[219]

MACHINERY

Machinery has been the pioneer of the world's progress.

—*James Ellis*

Machinery not only diffuses knowledge and distributes labor, but incites men to greater achievements.

—*Clough*

Machinery is an essential aid to human effort and to it we are indebted for manifold comforts and blessings which hand labor could not have bestowed.

—*John Pumfret*

STEAM

Steam is the wings of civilization.

—*John Todd*

Steam does for navigation what printing accomplishes for literature.

—*Acton*

In its present state the steam engine appears a thing most endowed with intelligence.

—*Arnott*

The application of steam to shipping deserves to be ranked among the greatest discoveries ever made.

—*Royal Robbins*

PHOTOGRAPHY

Photography is the art of immortalizing the dead.
—*Napoleon Sarony*

A photograph gives relief to the banished and absent lover.
—*James Iredell*

A photograph is a portrait painted by the sun.
—*Dupins*

PLOW

Plow deep and you will have plenty of corn.
—*Ewald*

Plow or not plow you must pay the rent.
—*Ewald*

The plow is the most valuable, and probably the most ancient, of all agricultural implements; there are traces of it in the earliest written authorities.
—*John Lauris Blake*

TABLE

Spread the table and contentions will cease.
—*Syra*

The table is as good a place to give instruction as a school-room.
—*Calvisius Jourus*

Utilities

There is no place where one's behavior is more observed than at the dinner table.

—*Henry Stephens*

SCHOOL

When schools flourish, all flourishes.

—*Luther*

School-houses are the republican line of fortifications.

—*Horace Mann*

The common schools are the very sources of a nation's intelligence.

—*J. Orville Taylor*

It is sufficient praise for our ancestors that they established schools.

—*David P. Page*

Odd Bunches

TRAMPS

I'll give a toast
To a strange host,
Who are to a man true topers, I think,
Here's to the tramps,
Those vagrant scamps,
Who drink what they can, and "can" what they
drink.

—Anon.

THE EPICURE

The epicure puts his purse into his belly.

—Anon.

THE HERMIT

When the devil grows old he turns hermit.

—Ariosto

A hermit is a deserter from the army of humanity.

—Southgate

THE MISER

The miser and the pig are of no use till dead.

—*La Mothe*

THE OFFICE BOY

A bumper to the Office Boy,
To whom all men are one;
He turns aside the millionaire,
He turns aside the bum!
Cerberus at the gates is he,
A lion in the path,
A hundred eyes are in his head,
But nary heart he hath.
Scowls he as your step draws near,
It's a sign for you to stop;
Nor tears nor gold will soften him,
For he knows he owns the shop.

—*R. W. Criswell*

BORES

There are some kind of men who cannot pass
their time alone; they are the bores of occupied
people.

—*L. G. A. Bonald*

A bore is a brainless, babbling button-holder.

—*Chatfield*

My experience of the world has shown me that
upon the whole, a bore gets on much better in it, and
is more respected and permanently popular than
what is called a clever fellow.

—*Dickens*

[224]

BEGGARS

Beggars! the only freemasons of the commonwealth; free, above scot-free, that observe no laws, obey no governor, use no religion, but what they draw from their own ancient custom, or constitute themselves; yet they are no rebels.

—*William Broome*

BACHELORS

Bachelors have a right to be fussy, especially old bachelors.

—*Fanny Fern*

A bachelor's time to marry never comes.

—*Thales*

CRITICS

I'll write, because I'll give
You critics means to live;
For should I not supply
The cause, th' effect would die.

—*Robert Herrick*

PIRATE'S SONG

A gallant ship, and a boundless sea,
A piping wind and the foe on our lee,
My pennon streaming so gay from the mast,
My cannon flashing all bright and fast.

—*Allan Cunningham*

THE PIRATE

Some fight, 'tis for riches; some fight, 'tis for fame;
The first I despise, and the last is a name.
I fight, 'tis for vengeance. I love to see flow,
At the strokes of my sabre, the life of my foe.

—Anon.

JACK'S ALIVE

Jack's alive, and a merry dog,
   When he gets on shore
He calls for his glass of grog,
   He drinks, and he calls for more.

Chorus

With a *whip, snip,* high cum diddledy,
   The cog-wheels of life have need of much oiling
Smack, crack,—this is our jubilee:
   Huzza, my lads! we'll keep the pot boiling.

—Frederick Marryat

JOLLY TAR

Here's to the jolly tar, that loves a beauty bright,
   And ofttimes thinks on her charms,
Who'll tease her with glee on a Saturday night,
   And wish him safe moored in her arms.

—Anon.

Some Dear Old Favorites

HER HEALTH!

I fill this cup to one made up
  Of loveliness alone,
A woman of her gentle sex
  The seeming paragon.
Her health! and would on earth there stood
  Some more of such a frame,
That life might be all poetry,
  And weariness a name.

          —Edward Coate Pickney

THE TRIUNE RULE

Here's to the Press, the Pulpit and the Petticoat,
he three ruling powers of the day
  The first spreads knowledge, the second spreads
norals, and the third spreads considerably.

          —Anon.

LET THE TOAST PASS

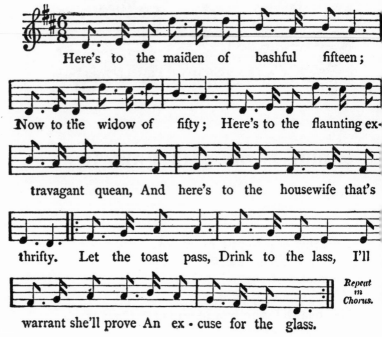

Here's to the maiden of bashful fifteen;
Now to the widow of fifty; Here's to the flaunting extravagant quean, And here's to the housewife that's thrifty. Let the toast pass, Drink to the lass, I'll warrant she'll prove An ex-cuse for the glass.

Repeat in Chorus.

Here's to the charmer whose dimples we prize,
　Now to the damsel with none, Sir,
Here's to the girl with a pair of blue eyes,
　And now to the nymph with but one, Sir.
　　Let the toast pass, etc.

Here's to the maid with a bosom of snow,
　Now to her that's as brown as a berry,
Here's to the wife with a face full of woe,
　And now to the damsel that's merry.
　　Let the toast pass, etc.

—*Sheridan*

THE BEAKER'S BRIM

Sparkling and bright in the liquid light,
  Does the wine our goblets gleam in;
With hue as red as the rosy bed
  Which a bee would choose to dream in.
Then fill to-night with hearts as light
  To loves as gay and fleeting
As bubbles that swim on the beaker's brim
  And break on the lips while meeting.
                    —*Charles Fenno Hoffman*

HERE'S TO THE GIRL

Here's to the girl with
  Eyes of blue,
Whose heart is kind and
  Love is true.

Here's to the girl with
  Eyes of brown,
Whose spirit proud you
  Cannot down.

Here's to the girl with
  Eyes of gray,
Whose sunny smile drives
  Care away.

Whate'er the hue of their
  Eyes may be,
I'll drink to the girls this
  Toast with thee!
                    —*Anon.*

[229]

HERE'S A HEART

Here's a sigh to those who love me,
   And a smile to those who hate,
And whatever sky's above me,
   Here's a heart for any fate.

—*Lord Byron*

COME ANY TIME

Come in the evening, or come in the morning—
Come when you're looked for, come without warning
A thousand welcomes you'll find here before you!
And the oftener you come the more I'll adore you!

—*Old Irish Toast*

A GOOD WISH

Here's a toast to all who are here,
No matter where you're from;
May the best day you have seen
Be worse than your worst to come.

—*Anon.*

THE WINE CUP

O, fill the wine cup high!
   The sparkling liquor pour;
For we will care and grief defy,
   They ne'er shall plague us more;
And ere the snowy foam
   From off the wine departs,
The precious draught shall find a home,
   A dwelling in our hearts.

—*Robert Folkstone Williams*

CLOVER CLUB'S TOAST

Here's to a long life and a merry one,
A quick death and a happy one,
A good girl and a pretty one,
A cold bottle and another one.

𝔖𝔬𝔪𝔢
𝔇𝔢𝔞𝔯 𝔒𝔩𝔡
𝔉𝔞𝔳𝔬𝔯𝔦𝔱𝔢𝔰

Origin of Toast-Masters

In the *City Press,* London, of June 4th, 1879, appeared the following:

"I recently heard, when dining in the city, that the origin of the custom of having toast-masters at city banquets was something as follows: It is said that at one of the banquets of the Old East India Company the Duke of Cambridge, who was always partial to dining in the city, had to speak. Mr. Toole, who was one of the officials of the company and a man by no means wanting in confidence, said: 'Some of the gentlemen have some difficulty in hearing your Royal Highness; shall I give out what the toast is?' The practice was found so convenient that it was repeated on many future occasions and Mr. Toole developed into the great 'City Toast-master.'"

Odd Old English Toasts

IN HONOR OF "MEASTER"

The last five lines here given as a "Dorsetshire Toast" form part of a toast or song that is usually the first done justice to at a Dorsetshire harvest home—that in honor of the "measter":

"Here's a health unto our master,
The founder of the feast,
And when that he is dead and gone
I hope his soul may rest.
I wish all things may prosper,
Whatever he takes his hand,
For we are all his servants
And serve at his command.
So drink! boys! drink!
And see that you do not spill,
For if you do
You shall drink two
'Tis by your master's will."

HERE'S TO YOU AND YOURS

Here's a health to you and yours who have done such things for us and ours; and when we and ours have it in our powers to do for you and yours what you and yours have done for us and ours, then we and ours *will* do for you and yours what you and yours have done for us and ours.

CLIMAX OF TOASTS

A wish having been expressed that the "Climax of Toasts" should be turned into a metrical form, as a mnemonic aid to diners-out—the following attempt is submitted to them:—

L'Abbé de Ville proposed a toast
His master as the rising *Sun*
Reisbach then gave the Empress Queen
As the bright *Moon* and much praise won.

The Earl of Stair, whose turn next came
Gave for his toast his own King Will
As Joshua the son of Nun
Who made both *Sun* and *Moon* stand still.

FRIENDSHIP AND LOVE

May the hinges of friendship never rust, or the wings of love lose a feather.

—*Old Scotch Toast*

GOOD LASS

Let the lass be good even if the glass is filled badly.

HEART

May woman's charm be dependent on neither eyes, hair nor complexion, but on heart.

GOOD CHEER

May the cold of Christmas be forgotten in the comfort of its cheer.

MERRY HEARTS

May all hearts be merry at Christmas, even when all hands are cold.

RESPECT

May we seek the society of women, but never chase her pleasure away.

OUR WINE

May our wine brighten the mind and strengthen the resolution.

WINE AND WISDOM

May Bacchus always be found to keep company with Solon.

MODESTY

May buoyant spirits never allow the ladies to forget their sex.

GOOD HEADS

May good heads be preferred to fine heads.

[235]

HAPPY STATE

May our slumbers be as light as fairy-steps and our conscience light as our sleep.

A HOPE

May woman's tears, like April showers, be succeeded by sunshine.

YOUNG LIFE

May the Spring-time of life never be visited by the Winter of despair.

HEARTS AND JOYS

May our hearts be light and our joys be quite independent of a heavy purse.

LOOKING BACKWARD

May the recollections of youth soften the ruggedness of manhood.

EARLY RISING

May we rise with the lark and participate in his lightness.

PRETTY LIKENESS

May our women resemble fairies in their spirits— never in their inconstancy.

STRAIGHT AND TRUE

May our sailors be constant as the needle and true as the compass.

PRESERVATION

May the beam in the glass never destroy the ray in the mind.

WHITE SECRET

May the bloom of the face never extend to the nose.

SANITY

May the wassail bowl never be the burial-place of our reason.

SOBER SUGGESTION

May we see so far before we commence drinking as to prevent our being blind when we have finished.

REWARD

May those who exert the industry of the bee, be like him, laden with riches.

FAIR EXCHANGE

May woman's trust ensure man's truth.

STEADY AND TRUE

May love be stronger than old wine, and ever discard the zephyr's wing.

FRIENDS

May mirth and reason, wit and wine, never be opposed to each other.

[237]

HEROES

May mankind never cease to produce heroes.

SOBRIETY

May we rise to behold the smiles of morning and retire with the shades of night.

MORNING LIGHT

May we seek the acquaintance of the "rising sun," that we may be introduced to " many days."

HIGH AND STRONG

May our spirits be like the lark; our principles like the oak.

GROWTH

May friendship, like wine, improve as time advances.

GOOD FRIENDS

May love and music be allies, never enemies.

PRUDENCE

May our imagination never run away with our judgment.

SOBER CUP

May the bumper of life be filled, but not with follies.

GOOD LUCK

May the last shilling soon have a successor.

Odd Old
English
Toasts

A GOOD BARGAIN

May we ever be able to part with our troubles to advantage.

FOREVER

May the braggart ever be cowed.

DECEPTION

May the ladies never be caught, like bees, by mere noise.

MAN'S FOLLY

May man's folly never tempt woman to wickedness.

AS IT SHOULD BE

May every lass have a lover and every lover become a husband.

SO SAY WE ALL

May injustice never make a rogue of an honest man.

TRUST

May we trust those we love, but never tempt them by neglect.

[239]

STRENGTH AND HABIT

May strength characterize our love and habit feed the flame.

FULFILLMENT

May we realize in dreams the presence of those who are away.

CONSOLATION

May the blighted heart find in every one a brother

WHITE MEMORIES

The spring-time of life: may the experience of age never destroy its purity of feeling.

FAITH

May neither time nor tide make us unfaithful, even if they make us unfortunate.

KEEP LOVE

May misfortune never compel a woman to be a wife without love.

DOUBT

May women begin to doubt when men begin to swear fidelity.

A TRIBUTE

May the warrior's rest relieve the warrior's ardor.

RECOGNITION

May we be pleased with all who strive to please us.

FETTERED FOLLY

May every fool be held with a tight hand.

BUSY NEST

May we each have so much business to mind as to make us leave our neighbors' alone.

CHAINS

May we show our good sense by controlling our senses.

MENTAL SHOWERS

May we not analyze, but purify our minds.

CLEAN HOUSE

May we analyze our own faults before we examine our neighbors'.

GOLDEN HOPE

Money!—may it ever be our friend, never our tyrant.

FREEDOM

May the maids have mistresses, not tyrants.

MISTRESS AND MAID

May liberality rule the mistress, modesty and industry characterize the maid.

[241]

LOCKJAW

When affection paints the portrait may critics' mouths be shut.

RESIGNATION

When Hope flies from our desires may our wishes accompany its flight.

THE EVERGREEN HOST

May farewells be forgotten, welcomes perpetuated.

STABILITY

May worth win hearts and constancy keep them.

THE CONSOLER

May long-standing sorrow be mellowed, if not removed, by time.

RESTFUL THOUGHT

May our bed never be harder than heather nor softer than feathers.

ON GUARD

May caution always be present during the vicinity of the foe.

CAUTION

When Fortune smiles may we never squander her favors.

FORTIFICATION

May the dreamy silence of evening prepare us for the stormiest scene of day.

IMAGINATION

May the imagination be ever ready to draw a moral from Nature's beauties.

SORROW AND HOPE

May woman's sorrow be as the dew, her hope warm as the sunshine.

FUTURE JOYS

May the hopes of Spring be realized in the Autumn of life.

NEW LIFE

May renewed hopes enable us to forget past disappointments.

PARTNERS

May the marriage bond banish every idea of rivalry in love.

PEACE

May jealousy never invade the domestic hearth.

ARMORED

May resolution disarm attacking omens.

[243]

HOPE'S ROSE

To the bloom of life's morning: may it never be roughly brushed away.

GOOD THOUGHT

May innocence in life ensure purity as life advances.

PRESERVATION

May the trophies of danger be watered with the tears of affection.

BEAUTY'S GIFT

May the smiles of beauty recompense the toils of the brave.

STIMULATION

May recollections of hope animate, and not dampen, exertion.

SOLACE

May the tears of affection, like the dew, never see a second sun.

GRANDEUR

May the contemplation of the majesty of the ocean dignify our minds.

PROGRESSION

Evening hours: may their quiet induce reflection, and reflection improve our hearts.

[244]

FIRST CALL
May love never make us forget duty.

HARMONY
May the wishes of the child harmonize with the duties of the mother.

A LONG ROAD
May the folly of the young be far away from the gray head.

FAITH
May we grasp present happiness without fear of future misery.

REWARD
May constancy secure kindness.

MEMORIES
May the remembrances of affection never depart.

EXPRESSION
May the feelings of the heart find vent through the tongue.

CONSIDERATION
May each man own a woman's love without forcing her to speak it.

DISAPPOINTMENTS
May young hopes learn to bear disappointments, but may they never invite them.

[245]

FOREARMED
May early rest prepare us for early rising.

WELCOME
May our wanderings from home never render less desirable our return to home.

UNITY
May courage ever be united with humanity.

HAPPY MOODS
Light hearts and light heels, merry tunes and a good piper.

IN TUNE
May the harmony of music never be a means of producing discord in the heart.

FREE TRADE
Trade: may it have freedom to range the world.

HARMLESS BULLS
May Paddy's bulls never be horned with mischief.

A MAN'S A MAN
May an old cloak never cover a ragged reputation.

REWARD
May perseverance be rewarded by prosperity.

FULFILLMENT
May the wanderer's visions of happiness be realized in his waking realities.

KINDNESS
May the maid's humility animate man's generosity.

SUNSHINE
May we never look from home to find that which may be gained at home.

THE MIRROR
May the smile on the face be but a reflection of the feeling of the heart.

A CLOAK
May the sunlight on the face never be a mask to conceal the sadness of the heart.

MIRTH
May the smile on the face be only of mirth, never of bitterness.

RECOGNITION
May the warrior's toils be rewarded by his country's gratitude.

DEFERENCE
May the discipline of the soldier never make him forget the rights of the citizen.

[247]

CARES AND PLEASURES

May zephyrs accompany our cares, fairies preside over our pleasures.

GOOD LUCK

May fortune favor enterprise.

MERIT

May the friends of our youth merit the regard of our age.

INSPIRATION

May the favor of the fair ensure firmness in fight.

SOBRIETY

May our wine gladden the heart, but not awaken the passions.

REALIZATION

May our wine add wings to Old Time, but not make us insensible to his flight.

GOOD NATURE

May hilarity always be united with temperance.

FIDELITY

May our father's song remind us only of his virtues.

JUDGMENT

May the good old songs render us better able to estimate the merits of the new.

HARMONY
May riches never destroy heart.

BENEVOLENCE
May our friends help us to enjoy wealth and may the poor partake of our superfluity.

LOYALTY
May each lass have a true lover.

TRUST
When women believe, may men never deceive

ALLIANCE
May trust ever be allied with truth.

TEMPERANCE
May discretion preside over our cups.

CONTROL
May the joys of drinking never supersede the pleasure of reasoning.

HAPPY STATE
May innocence ever be allied to happiness.

RESTING PLACES
May fair bosoms be the habitations of pure hearts.

[249]

CLEAN HEARTS

May fair clothes always cover fair hearts.

STABILITY

May the lover's pride be succeeded by the husband's truth and affection.

FAIR AND FOUL

May fair faces never tempt to foul morality.

PRINCIPLES

May our maidens patronize principles rather than persons.

DIGNITY

May the coquetry of the maiden be abandoned when she assumes the station of wife.

PATIENCE

May the wife's trifling never be stronger than her husband's patience.

GUIDE-POSTS

May brave hearts be guided by clear heads.

BLESSINGS

May susceptible hearts be blessed with firm principles.

A KING

May the time arrive when every serf shall determine to be a man.

GOOD SPIRIT

May the spirit of generosity never be dampened by the blight of ingratitude.

FALSE IMPRESSIONS

May noise never excite us to battle, nor confusion reduce us to defeat.

PEACEFUL SUNS

May our suns set in peace, even if they rise to witness our toil.

FERRYMAN

May the ferryman have a good boat, a stout arm, and a steady heart.

TOP-HEAVY

May the head be never so heavy as to capsize the boat.

OPEN FIGHTER

May we be open to enemies, but do deeds of friendship in secret.

A CLEAN BOOK

May the laurels of the brave never be sullied by Indian treachery.

RECOGNITION

May long service secure strong promotion.

[251]

PASSIONS

May we never gratify our passions at the expense of another's feelings.

LONGEVITY

May length of life ensure strength of wisdom.

LIVES

May we enjoy our lives without spending them.

DISCIPLINE

May we never allow any servants to become our masters.

HUNTER'S TOAST

A good steed, a good stag, a high scent, a strong pack, and a stout heart.

HOPE

When Adversity assaults, may Hope interpose its hand.

ADAPTABILITY

May we share our luxuries with our friends and ever be ready to share in their distress.

WANTS

May our wants be so few as to enable us to relieve the wants of our friends.

CARES AND COMFORTS

May the sailor's cares be driven away by the winds, his comforts be firm as his planks.

RESPECT

May the name of woman ensure respect, her presence inspire it.

RAINBOW

A stout ship, a clear sea, and a far-off coast in stormy weather.

WANTS

May our wants be subjected to our reason.

AGE AND YOUTH

May age ensure wisdom; youth, innocence.

PLEASURE

May pleasure never tempt us to forget that night was made for repose, day for action.

EYE AND BRAIN

While our wine brightens the eye, may it never burden the brain.

WARMTH

May the bottle inspire warmth, but never sufficient heat to fire us.

WIT

May our wit never be dependent upon wine.

JUSTICE

May punishment attend idleness, fortune accompany exertion.

MATRIMONY

May matrimony stimulate to honest exertion and to industry.

LIGHT HEARTS

May care never cause us to abandon innocent amusement.

REWARD

May unjust jealousy prove its own punishment.

NATIVE HEATH

May the experience of the wanderer endear to him more firmly his native home.

BYGONE DAYS

May foreign pleasures never banish from the mind a relish for home scenes.

SORROWS AND HOPES

May the sorrows of the fair be evanescent as the dew, their hopes bright as the sun.

SAILOR'S SUPPORT

May courage inhabit the sailor's breast and danger nerve his heart.

FRIENDS

May our friends be in our hearts, whether they be remembered in wine or water.

A BREEZY THOUGHT

The wind that blows, the ship that goes, and the lass that loves a sailor.

THE BETTER HALF

May woman be our companion; may we never make her a slave.

THE BRAVER HALF

Woman, may she ever remain the guard of man's virtue.

A GOOD HOPE

May each innocent heart be gifted with a cautious head.

FORTITUDE

May sorrow never induce a resort to wine.

CARE AND REASON

Let us never attempt to lighten care by drowning reason.

WANT AND CARE

May want never drive the gipsy out of the pale or within the grasp of the law.

[255]

RECOMPENSE

May man's gratitude never fail to recompense a brute's kindness.

WORDS

May the words of the absent be more fully cherished than if spoken if they were present.

ENJOYMENT

May personal enjoyment never make us forget those who depend on us for place.

INSPIRATION

May the old mariner's stories impart enterprise to young seamen.

DUTY

May remembrance of an absent home never divert a sailor from his duty.

COMFORT

May the old man's loneliness be soothed by the consideration of the young.

TOWN AND COUNTRY

Woodland pleasures: may they never be associated with town vice.

NATURE'S GEMS

The beauties of nature: may our hearts never become callous to their influence.

JOYS AND SPIRITS

Harmless joys, with spirits to enjoy them.

A HAPPY HOPE

May the merry day's actions never be succeeded
by the next day's regret.

FEASTS

May the feasts which bind old Christmas open all
hearts to the poor.

SPEED THE PLOUGH

May God speed the plough and reward the men
who drive it.

STAFF OF LIFE

May they who raise the wheat be well rewarded
by plenty.

VILLAGE BELLS

If the village bells sadden the mind, may the simplicity of their sounds tend to purify the heart.

MEMORIES AND REFLECTIONS

The village bells, may their sounds awaken
the memories of the past and open the heart to
reflection.

MAN AND BRUTE

May man's passions never make him forget that
the brute has feelings.

[257]

DAILY TOIL

May the toils of the day be forgotten in the welcome of night.

GLADNESS AND REPOSE

May the spring-time of gladness be succeeded by the winter-time of repose.

HEADS AND HEARTS

When our hearts are merry may our heads be active.

DOUBLE TROUBLE

May she who would have two lovers be punished by double contempt.

VIRTUES

May we wear our own clothes, but adopt any person's virtues.

PRIDE AND PASSION

May pride never intrude on a wedding day, nor passion interrupt its harmony.

A BRIDAL WISH

May a bridal promise never be repented, nor the matrimonial bond regretted.

MERRY HEARTS

Merry hearts to village maidens.

ENGLISH SPORTS

Old English sports, may they never be done away with.

ENGLISH CUSTOMS

Old English customs, may modern refinement never introduce habits less healthful.

A HOPE

May empty heads never disgrace our country's cockade.

HEARTS AND PLANTS

May hearts of oak man our navy, and plants of oak support it.

FRIENDSHIPS

May our friendships be independent of time and be matured by character.

GOOD FORTUNE

May just wars be accompanied by good fortune.

TOPER

May a quarrelsome toper be compelled to be a teetotaler.

NOSEGAY

May we never color the nose by emptying the pocket.

[259]

REWARD

May he who parts with his last shilling to relieve distress never know what it is to want it.

REALIZATION

May the dreams of the warrior return him to his home.

COMPLETE HAPPINESS?

Lots of beef, oceans of beer, a pretty girl and a thousand a year.

TRUTH

May truth animate Paddy's heart when blarney stimulates his tongue.

FULL TUMBLER

A full tumbler to every good fellow, a good tumble to every bad one.

ROSE, THISTLE AND SHAMROCK

The rose, thistle and shamrock, may they never be disunited.

PAST AND PRESENT

May we never abandon present happiness by looking back on past circumstances.

ON HAND

May the midnight of the mind find all willing to illuminate its darkness

PEEP O' DAY

May the rising sun and the lark's song be our morning visitors.

HARMONY

May the nightingale's song harmonize the feelings of our hearts.

TRANQUILLITY

May the shadows of evening calm the excitement of the day.

LOVE AND SONG

May our love be like good wine, grow stronger as it grows older.

GOLD

May gold never guide our opinions.

JUSTICE

May she who encourages two lovers at one time lose both.

MISER

May he who pleads poverty to save his pocket soon find it empty.

MONEY

May money never prevent love and never buy it.

BLUSHES

May we witness the blushes of the morning, that we may hope to participate in its bloom.

TEARS

May the tears of affection, like the dew, never see a second sun.

DREAMS

May we never allow dreams to be omens unless they predict happiness.

WITHOUT MASK

May we never receive an old friend with a new face.

OLD DAYS

May prosperity never make us forget the friends of our adversity.

HOSPITALITY

May we never want a friend or a glass to give him.

DIGNITY
May our dignity be independent of our station.

"LEST WE FORGET"
May riches never destroy heart.

ALLIANCE
May friendship propose the toast, and sincerity drink it.

HARMONY
May harmony fill our hearts and not merely charm our ears.

OFF THE KEY
May the sons of discord never be introduced among the children of song.

BRAINS
May each witty story bear a good moral, and may we have brains to find it.

BUMPS
May our actions be right, even if phrenologists say we have bad heads.

WHY WORRY?

May our meetings never be saddened by the prospect of parting.

REVERIE AND REPOSE

The dreamy hours of moonlight; may we be calm enough to enjoy them.

THE WILD HEART

May the heart that is as wild as the bird never be caught in the snare of despair.

PUNISHMENT

May coquetry receive the reward of heartlessness.

INDULGENCE

May mothers never spoil their pets.

BORES

May pets never become pests.

HIDDEN ENEMIES

May young hearts never be a prey to old cares.

HUSBAND-HUNTERS

May husband-hunters find themselves over-matched.

FOLLIES

May our hearts never be oppressed by the follies of fashion.

[264]

FEAR

May we never meet misfortune half way by anticipating her movements.

STRENGTH

May resolution animate us to resist weak regrets.

NEW LIFE

May the sorrows of the exile recede as he leaves the scene of their origin.

SIRE AND SON

May the son's conduct never dishonor the sire's gray hairs.

LIFE'S REWARD

May old age be honored and its experience revered.

FRIENDS

May the conduct of our friends during trials prove them worthy of the name.

THE SLEEPY-HEAD

May we sleep for rest, not to indulge sloth.

HEAVEN ON EARTH

May our love be a fairy in spirits, an angel in her principles.

CUPID'S CALENDAR

Love's almanac: may it be a perpetual one.

[265]

BUD AND BLOSSOM

May pure hopes spring like the verdure and blossom as the flowers.

SIMPLICITY

May we prize our country's plainness before the beauty of a foreign strand.

FRESH OUTLOOK

May the memory of past blessings preserve a hope of future fortune.

REWARDS

May hard labor secure strong health.

HEARTS

May our hearts never be fired by mere beauty.

DUTY

May duty ever rise superior to inclination.

TWILIGHT

May the quiet hours of the brave be shared by the fair.

TRUE LOVE

May the heart that doth truly love never be despised.

THE GREEN EYE

May suspicion never mar the lover's happiness.

[266]

BUOYANCY

In the gloomiest hour may our spirits rise upon the wings of hope.

LOVE'S ENERGY

May obstacles in the path of love be removed by love's energy.

LOVE AND DUTY

May nothing divert us from our love, and may our love never divert us from our duty.

GRIEF

May grief be as the morning cloud, but may it never leave without chastening the heart.

SURVIVAL

May the warmth of our affections survive the frosts of age.

AWAKENINGS

May the dreams of our boyhood be forgotten in the realities of our maturity.

THE PAST

May we never sigh after past pleasures, or mourn after past pains.

HOSPITALITY

May the exile's sorrow be forgotten in the smiles of a foreign strand.

[267]

GOSSIPS

May gossips prove torments to themselves by finding no food for scandal.

EMPTY HOUSE

May scandal-mongers never find listeners.

FAIRY FLIGHTS

May traditions never do more harm than the legend of the Flying Dutchman.

SANITY

May music amuse, but not madden.

INDEPENDENCE

May our happiness never be dependent upon place or pocket.

INFLEXIBILITY

May we never bend our reason to our inclinations.

TIT FOR TAT

May a good joke always inspire a smart rejoinder.

COMFORT

May we imagine our situations better, rather than worse, than our neighbors'.

LITTLE DEVILS

May trifling obstacles never obstruct pleasure.

[268]

BRAVERY

May danger stimulate to, and never deter from, duty.

OBSTACLES

May obstacles entice enterprise and ensure perseverance.

—W. J. Marchant,
in "Notes and Queries"

Miscellaneous Toasts

Triumphant eloquence that knows no depth,
Or height or width yet unattained—
Abject before your fiery strength we bow—
Spellbound—by glowing metaphor enchained.
Toward thee direct'd our strongest tribute is but weak
Since tongues of men, not hearts, must speak.

—*Henry Stanley Haskins*

TOAST AND ROAST

When T stands for tender
And R stands for rough
You've the difference twixt a
Toast and a Roast—
Sure enough.

—*Stanlicus*

BASHFULNESS

Of all our parts, the eyes express
The sweetest kind of bashfulness.

—*Robert Herrick*

ROYALLY MELLOW

A toast to the fellow
  Who when he drinks deep
Gets royally mellow
  And then falls asleep.
But not to the varlet
  Who as he grows tight,
Turns noisy and scarlet
  And starts in to fight.
                    —*Wm. E. S. Fales*

SUB-ROSA

Here's to the girl, demure and bland,
  In entertaining, apt and able;
Whose eyes look down, whene'er her hand
  Caresses yours beneath the table.
                    —*Wm. E. S Fales*

CLUB vs. HOME

Here's to our home,
  And here's to our club,
But not to the home
  Where the club waits the "hub."
                    —*Phil McAllister*

EVENING

What time the sun
Threw from far-distant hills a lengthened shade,
Lifting the yoke from the o'er-labored steer,
Saying, as sank his orb, "Rejoice, thy task is done."
                    —*Horace*

[271]

MONK'S TOAST

I'll praise your hair, your eyes, your brow,
Sing hey, sing ho, sing heydy!
   I'd splinter lances for your sake,
   'Twere better lance than heart should break.
   But lack-and-a-day, what art can make
A knight of a monk, my lady?

        —Robert Emmet Mac Alarney,
           from "Ye Mayde of Yorke"

FATHER TIME

Exasperating and everlasting white shadow! Thou
flagman on every man's "Limited!" You'll have to
keep on cutting grass until the end of your title; and
when that comes to pass where will you be?

        —Pseud.

KILKENNY

O! the boys of Kilkenny are brave roving blades,
And if ever they meet with the nice little maids,
They'll kiss them, and coax them, and spend their
    money free,
Of all the towns in Ireland Kilkenny for me.

        —Anon.

MIRTH

Crowned with clusters of the vine,
Let us sit, and quaff our wine.
Call on Bacchus, chant his praise;
Shake the thyrse, and bite the bays.

        —Robert Herrick

HONOR

Honor is so sublime perfection,
And so refined, that when God was alone
And creatureless at first, Himself had none.
—*John Donne*

TIBUR

Tibur's groves and orchards dewed by rills
That dance their glad way down from Tibur's
wooded hills.
—*Horace*

MERE MAN

The thing about mere man which impresses me
most, which fills me with the greatest respect, is
not his courage in the face of death, but the courage
with which he faces life.
—*Sarah Grand*

HER HAIR

Her hair the net of golden wire
Wherein my heart, led by my wandering eyes,
So fast entangled is that in no wise
It can, nor will, again retire.
—*Thomas Bateson*

THE ONSET

Sound! bid your terrible trumpets bray!
Blow till their brazen throats give way!
Sound to the battle! Sound I say!
Huzzah! Huzzah!
—*Barry Cornwall*

YOUTH

Drink wine, and live here blitheful, while ye may:
The morrow's life too late is; live to day.
—*Robert Herrick*

HEARTS OF OAK

We ne'er see our foes but we wish them to stay,
They never see us but they wish us away;
If they run, why we follow, or run them ashore;
For if they won't fight us we cannot do more.
—*Garrick*

REPUTATION

Reputation is life itself.
—*Zchwartz*

Reputation is a great inheritance.
—*Seneca*

Reputation is one of the attributes of virtue.
—*James Ellis*

VERSES

Who will not honor noble numbers, when
Verses outlive the bravest deeds of men?
—*Robert Herrick*

MYSTERY

Take the mystery out of things and they lose
two-thirds of their attraction.
—*H. W. Shaw*

MYSTERY

There is a profound charm in mystery.

—*Chatfield*

A religion without its mysteries is a temple without a God.

—*Robert Hall*

It is the dim haze of mystery that adds enchantment to pursuit.

—*Rivarol*

SUPREMEST BEAUTY

If when the sun at noon displays
His brighter rays,
Thou but appear,
He then, all pale with shame and fear,
Quencheth his light,
Hides his dark brow, flies from thy sight,
And grows more dim.

—*Thomas Carew*

SANTA CLAUS

O, roly-poly, twinkling-eyed, laughing-sided character! You're the finest old fraud that ever came out of the imagination. What a population of "press agents" you have all over the world! And how you do "make good." What stories you have inspired! What memories of thee have floated through the turn-pike of Toyland! What pictures of thy funny "make up" have been painted!

Live forever!—old chap.

—*Pseud.*

[275]

TEARS

Tears, though they're here below the sinner's brine,
Above they are the angels' spiced wine.

—*Robert Herrick*

A WISH

Health to enjoy the blessings sent
From heaven; a mind unclouded, strong;
A cheerful heart; a wise content;
An honored age; and song.

—*Horace*

TO A HESITATING TOASTER

Give the toast, my good fellow; be jovial and gay,
And let the brisk moments pass jocund away!

—*Anon.*

HERE'S HOPING

Here's hoping your life may be happy and gay,
Some honest work done, and some leisure for play.
A bride and a baby to worship divine,
Long pipes on verandas where wild roses climb.
And last—since I'm toasting your happiness true—
Here's hoping—here's hoping your friends may be
few.

—*Robert Emmet Mac Alarney*

MODERATION

In things a moderation keep;
Kings ought to shear, not skin, their sheep.

—*Robert Herrick*

[**276**]

ACROSS THE SEA

To our brothers across the ocean,
    To the days of long ago,
        To the tale we bring,
        To the song we sing,
And the friends that we used to know.
                            —*Old Toast*

HER EYES

Clear are her eyes,
Like purest skies,
Discovering from thence
A baby there
That turns each sphere,
Like an Intelligence.
                    —*Robert Herrick*

TO CONQUER

Hearts of oak are our ships, jolly tars are our men,
        We always are ready,
        Steady, boys, steady,
We'll fight and we'll conquer again and again.
                            —*Anon.*

GLEAMING EYES

Oh, blue is the drooping sky above,
And blue are the eyes that gleam,
And low her laugh as I eager quaff
The draught of a happy dream.
                —*Robert Emmet Mac Alarney*

[**277**]

DEVOTION

O Jupiter, should I speak ill
Of woman-kind, first die I will;
Since that I know, 'mong all the rest
Of creatures, woman is the best.

—*Robert Herrick*

CLEVERNESS

Here's to the clever;
May they be with us ever.

—*Meusa*

CASTLES IN THE AIR

A sigh can shatter a castle in the air.

—*Alger*

Ah! castles in the air cost a great deal to keep up.
—*Bulwer*

If you have built castles in the air your work
need not be lost; that is where they should be.
Now put the foundations under them.

—*Thoreau*

BY PROXY

I dare not ask a kiss,
  I dare not beg a smile,
Lest having that, or this,
  I might grow proud the while.

No, no, the utmost share
  Of my desire shall be
Only to kiss that air
  That lately kissed thee.

—*Robert Herrick*

[278]

HAPPINESS

That happiness does still the longest thrive,
Where joys and griefs have turns alternative.

—Robert Herrick

MERRINESS

Let's now take our time
While we're in our prime,
And old, old age is afar off;
For the evil, evil days
Will come on apace,
Before we can be aware of.

—Robert Herrick

TO HOPE

Sweet Hope, ethereal balm upon me shed,
And wave thy silver pinions o'er my head.
Peep with the moonbeams through the leafy roof,
And keep that fiend, Despondence, far aloof.

—John Keats

CONTENTMENT

If those who drain the shepherd's bowl
  No high and sparkling wines can boast;
With wholesome cups they cheer the soul,
  And crown them with the village toast.

—James Thomson

THE BODY

The body is the soul's poor house or home,
Whose ribs the laths are, and whose flesh the loam.

—Robert Herrick

FULL VALUE

If little labor, little are our gains;
Man's fortunes are according to his pains.
—*Robert Herrick*

PEACE

Around us all is Peace: the steer
Crops the lush pasture of the lea.
—*Horace*

The End of the Play

The play is done; the curtain drops,
    Slow falling to the prompter's bell;
A moment yet the actor stops,
    And looks around, to say farewell.
It is an irksome word and task;
    And, when he's laughed and said his say,
He shows, as he removes the mask,
    A face that's anything but gay.

One word, ere yet the evening ends,
    Let's close it with a parting rhyme,
And pledge a hand to all young friends,
    As fits the merry Christmas time.
On life's wide scene you, too, have parts,
    That Fate ere long shall bid you play;
Good night! with honest, gentle hearts
    A kindly greeting go alway!

Good-night!—I'd say, the griefs, the joys,
    Just hinted in this mimic page,
The triumphs and defeats of boys,
    Are but repeated in our age.
I'd say your woes were not less keen,
    Your hopes more vain than those of men;
Your pangs or pleasures of fifteen
    At forty-five played o'er again.

                —*Thackeray*

L'Envoi

Come, love and health to all;
Then I'll sit down.   Give me some wine, fill full,
I drink to the general joy o' the whole table.
                                        —*Shakespeare*

Reserved for Additional Original Toasts

Note:—The following pages are left
blank for the purchaser's convenience, to
be devoted, by him, to original toasts or to
those gathered at dinners. The publishers
offer a first prize of $10.00, a second prize
of $7.00 and a third prize of $5.00 for the
best original toasts not exceeding eight lines
each. They will pay $3.00 each for accept-
able toasts submitted in the competition.
Address MSS. to Rohde & Haskins, 16
Cortlandt Street, New York, New York,
U. S. A.

Reserved for Additional Original Toasts

Reserved for Additional Original Toasts

Reserved for Additional Original Toasts

Reserved for Additional Original Toasts

Reserved for Additional Original Toasts

Reserved for Additional Original Toasts

Reserved for Additional Original Toasts

Reserved for Additional Original Toasts

Reserved for Additional Original Toasts

Reserved for Additional Original Toasts

Reserved for Additional Original Toasts

Index to Authors

Index to Authors

Index
to Authors